Welcome, dear readers!

The theme for this issue is 'A Splash of Colour" and spring is the perfect time to brighten things up! As always our Pretty Nostalgic Compendium is written with the help of our fellow Nostalgianeer members and although none of us are paid professionals, we hope you will appreciate our heartfelt efforts as we share with you our passion for the past.

This issue we recount the fascinating wartime memories of June Farquhar von Schmiderer, who once bumped into Churchill in her dressing gown! We meet Kaffe Fassett, the most colourful man in textiles; we take you on a tour of two magnificent hand-painted period properties; we show you how to add colour to your own home with vintage style embroidery and window seats; we inspire you to create gloriously fancy footwear with decoupage; we teach you how to recreate authentic Victorian curries and hopefully ignite a passion for classic 1930s detective novels - and that's not all!

We would love to hear from you, dear readers, we value your opinions and comments on our publications and we would especially love to hear about the things we have inspired you to make or do, especially if you have some photographs to show us too. Also you are welcome to join us as a Nostalgianeer and membership can include either digital or print copies of our books.

Wishing you many happy days from vintage ways,

Nicole X

Nicole Burnett
Founder and Editor Pretty Nostalgic and The Nostalgianeers
nicole@prettynostalgic.co.uk

CONTENTS

CURIOSITIES

Infusing freshly opened hawthorn blossoms in brandy, with a little sugar, can make a fragrant liqueur. The liqueur is strained and bottled after 3 months. This is seldom drunk alone but usually added to other drinks for flavouring. Hawthorn is also a good heart tonic.

MAKE A LITTLE BIRD HOUSE IN YOUR SOUL

You can make a nesting box for our feathered friends out of anything, no need to buy one specially, just use a bit of imagination and take a closer look at the bits and pieces you have hanging around.

This clever teapot house is perfect, the lid can be removed at the end of the summer to allow thorough cleaning and it is hardwearing, water and wind proof so the little chicks will be comfortable until they fledge.

When making the entrance hole, make sure it is at least 125 mm from the floor of the nesting box otherwise the young birds may fall out or worse, be scooped out by a cat. Also a roughened surface below the entrance hole should help the young birds to clamber up when it's time for them to leave.

The size of the entrance hole depends on the type of bird you wish to attract, small holes of 25 mm will entice blue, coal and marsh tits, while a larger hole of 32 mm will be preferred by house sparrows and nuthatches.

Dew diligence

Our ancestors took the threat of damp evening air very seriously as it was said to be full of exhalations from the earth, and therefore injurious to health.

*"The dews of the evening
Carefully shun;
They're the tears of the earth
For the loss of the sun."*

When Shadows fall.

Pass a smile along

Some sterling advice given out to ladies during the First World War – This positive attitude helped us get through a horrid war and still holds fast today.

"Be optimistic, let us believe in the best of possibilities and determine to swim up-stream. The feeling given out and looked for is reflected in others, and undoubtedly one is taken at one's own valuation. A kind and encouraging word to others, a helping hand, a cheery laugh, are all aids to spirit of confidence, and an inducement to others to smile in the face of trouble, and to pass the smile along."

LAMB'S TAIL PIE

This was a great delicacy made at lambing times when the lamb's tails are docked for hygiene reasons. The tails were cleaned and freed from scraps of wool, scalded, cut into pieces, put into a pie dish with a little piece of mint, salt and pepper, and covered with a good crust made from mutton fat.

5

CURIOSITIES

LEAVE YOUR MARK

We visited William Morris's Red House which you can read all about on page 16 and discovered a great way of recording the history of your home and preserving it for prosterity. Guests to the house, mostly after Morris sold it in 1865, were encouraged to engrave their signatures on a glazed screen in the porch. One hundred and six names were inscribed over the years and some of the visitors were very famous and influential such as Willaim Morris' daughter May and Arthur Lasenby Liberty, the founder of the famous London store. Today these simple scratches form a fascinating record of the house's comings and goings. You may not have such notable visitors but it is still a lovely idea, even if you use a more conventional visitors book instead.

Mint Jelly

Make your Easter Lamb lunch special. Mint sauce makes a vital contribution to the perfect lamb dinner and by serving it as individual Easter inspired portions, it will bring a smile too.

Take 1 cupful of granulated sugar. 1 cupful of vinegar, ¾ cupful of finely chopped fresh green mint. Soak 1 tablespoonful of gelatine with cold water for ½ an hour, boil the sugar and vinegar together until they thicken then add the soaked gelatine, and stir until dissolved, add the chopped mint and seasoning and stir until it begins to boil, and the mint ceased to rise. Pour into tiny wetted pots or moulds and turn out when set. Can be served with hot or cold lamb.
Cassells Household Guide 1912

Pink Pancakes

Pink Pancakes make a pretty dish for a spring breakfast, and are simple to make.

Peel and pound a large beetroot in a mortar. It must be well cooked but a good colour. When it is a smooth paste, add 3 oz of flour, 1 gill of cream, ¼ of a teaspoonful of grated nutmeg. 2oz of castor sugar, yolks of 4 well-beaten eggs, and ½ a wineglass (2 fluid oz) of brandy. Fry them in little cakes in butter.

HOME MADE BLACK JACK

Black Jack is an old fashioned name for gravy browning. Very simply, it's a dark liquid of burnt sugar, and was always made at home. If bottled it keeps for many years. This recipe comes from a lovely Victorian cook book called 'Dainty Dishes for Slender Incomes' and it is good for colouring all sorts of dishes, including stews and casseroles.

"Put some brown sugar in a stewpan with a little water, and allow it to boil until it becomes black and the vapour that arises is quite white, then add a little water to make it again liquid, boil up, strain off into a jar for use."

Put a cork in it!

Instead of throwing away old corks, it is worthwhile to collect them in a box because they can be very useful while spring-cleaning.

" A cork dipped in paraffin is effective in removing rust from metal and stains from lamp glasses and hearth-tiles, while disfiguring marks on polished wood and also on wallpaper and window-panes will often yield to treatment with a dry cork. Stains on aluminium and enamelled saucepans can be removed by means of cork dipped in salt and kitchen knives, together with any cutlery not made of stainless steel, are best treated with moistened cork, rubbed along a bar of household soap. Burnt marks on plates can be removed by means of a cork dipped in a little damp salt; spots on linoleum disappear when rubbed with a cork repeatedly dipped in petrol."

Fishing for corks
For this a small staple is inserted in a number of corks, and each player is provided with a miniature fishing rod, made from a small stick, and some strong thread with a bent pin as a hook.

LIFE STORIES
JUNE FARQUHAR VON SCHMIDERER

SIBYLLE LAUBSCHER from Switzerland
shares the remarkable memories of an
extraordinary British lady who helped
smuggle family jewels out of Nazi Germany
and met Churchill in her dressing gown

June

When I was living in Vienna, I was assigned
to June as her "young visitor" by the Anglican
Church there. June was living on her own near
Schönbrunn and the idea was to bring some
more life into her routine as her knees were
no longer up to long walks or going anywhere
much. In retrospect, I'm not quite sure who
profited most, she became my "third granny"
and I had the opportunity to learn about her
amazing life. After countless cups of tea and
listening to her stories "before the war"…
"after the war", I declared this was too good,
and I would write her life story down. So
began our weekly routine: I would turn up with
my notebook and empty tapes, make us a pot of
tea and sit down to listen to her story.

SECRET

Cypher M/1939.
Reporting Code (1931).
Interdepartmental Cypher (1936)

SECRET.

CYPHER MESSAGE.

To—

INFORMATION.

Date

Receipt   Despatch

Time of

I, JUNE FARQUHAR VON SCHMIDERER, was born on 13th February 1921 in Sydney, Australia. My mother, Amy was born in 1891 in Australia and my father, Philip in 1878 in India. My father's father was born in England and fell in love with a young lady on board ship during his first journey out to India at the age of 22. My grandmother was on board, having been rescued from a ship, also on its way to India, which sank in the Mediterranean. By the time my father was born, my grandfather had tea plantations in southern India. My father was sent back to England for his education, to a very spartan public school as they were in those days. Daddy was totally tone deaf, but his parents thought it would be a good idea if he played the violin. He shared a room with Thomas Beecham (from the liver pill family) and Thomas became so

fed-up he snatched the violin out of Daddy's hands and broke it over his head. Thomas Beecham later became a famous conductor.

My mother, growing up in Australia, took a trip to Fiji to visit some relatives. Before leaving she visited a fortune teller who told her she would fall in love with a fair, wavy-haired young man on the Fiji boat. It all came true. They were married in Sydney in 1920. At this time, Philip was working in the sugar plantations in Fiji. When I was born my mother went home to her parents to have me and we returned to Fiji for about a year. Then my father moved to Australia importing tea and coffee from India.

My first experience of the cinema was the "Broadway Melodies" in the late 1920s. *Tarzan of the Apes* was the first film I saw

when I was about 10. The animals in the jungle terrified me!

My brother, Richard, was born on 29th March 1924. We both attended school from the age of 5 – a small private school about 15 minutes up the road towards the railway station of Killara on the North Shore Line. There was a dancing mistress who came every week to give classical dance classes – I loved it and always wanted to take up dancing as a career, but they said I couldn't because I was too tall. I was almost the same height as I am now – 5 ft 10½ at the age of 12! Miss Hill, one of the mistresses, married an Englishman just before we left Australia for England. We gave her a goodbye present (an umbrella!) thinking we would never see her again. Then, when we were settled in Crawley Down near East Grinstead, we were walking down the high

June's passport

street one day, whom should we bump into but Miss Hill, now Mrs Wood!

We didn't have a car in Australia. My Aunt Dorothy had a car, which my mother learnt to drive, but my father could only ride a horse. Aunt Dorothy sent her daughter Ann to boarding school in England for a year in 1930. We were all most impressed because she'd seen the Queen. Ann told us how pupils lined up in their red cloaks when the Royal Family drove past, saying "now I can put my elbows on the table, as I've seen the Queen."

There was a great depression in Sydney at the beginning of the 1930s and my father became increasingly frustrated. People fed-up with the left-wing governor started a political group called the New Guard in 1931. The movement appealed to conservative returned servicemen who were strongly anti-communist and deeply suspicious of the Labour Premier of New South Wales. My father joined this guard and they had shooting practise down the bottom of our garden. When the new Sydney Harbour Bridge was opened the Honourable John T. Lang was to officially declare it open, but instead the Captain of the New Guard rode up and slashed the ribbon with his sword and declared it open in the name of the people of Sydney.

My father decided to sell up in 1933 and return to England, which he had last seen when he was at school there. My mother had last seen England in 1911, when she'd travelled there with her family, aged 11.

We had a lovely six-week trip to England on the '*Largs Bay*', later used as a troop ship during the war and finally sank. I didn't like being in Australia as a child, it was terrifying for me, the only thing I liked was the sea, I think.

My father was thinking what kind of business he should start, when he saw a new fangled dry-cleaning system for clothes, called a Burtol, in London. You could have your clothes cleaned (using trichloroethylene), pressed and ready for collection within six hours. The firm was run by retired admirals, and he thought "if admirals can run dry-cleaning businesses, so can I". We settled in Crawley Down, and my father's dry-cleaning business was quite successful during the war as people were unable to buy new clothes.

My mother met some pleasant people who recommended a school for me on the other side of Gatwick, St. Joan's School. After Mrs Waller's daughter left school I caught the steam train, then the bus to and from school. On Thursdays the train used to stop at Gatwick because it was "Race Day". There was a famous racecourse there, used by the Canadian Air Force to repair and maintain planes during the war, and turned into Gatwick airport afterwards.

Leaving Australia - June, brother Richard and mother, Amy

June's father Philip in the garden

English school days

Christel and June in Trafalgar Square

It was very difficult to get used to school in England to start with. On hearing I came from Australia, they used to say, "but you're white! There are only Aborigines living in Australia!" Richard, at a boy's prep school was bullied about his Australian accent and called a convict.

There was a very nice girl at school from Hagen in Westphalia, Germany. She looked after the younger children and was great fun, so I thought I would like to learn German. Consequently she taught me German and I decided to go to Germany for six months. She arranged for me to go to stay with a German family in Hagen on leaving school.

But before that I departed for a holiday with Aunt Cora, my father's sister. She rented a very posh house in Chester Street in the centre of London, not far from Buckingham Palace, where she let out rooms (which she wasn't allowed to) to various Australians over on visits. Aunt Cora was a great character and she took us to see the Folies Bergere in Paris as we had

to wait for the night train to Rome. The first time I saw all these almost naked ladies on stage with just feathers in front of them, it was great fun. We stayed in Capri for a week, during which time I ate veal for the very first time.

We came back to England from Capri – the whole trip cost GBP 11 in those days – 10 days for 11 Pounds, amazing. The political situation in Europe was worsening, but Chamberlin met Hitler in Bonn and "peace in our time" was declared. So in September I set off for Germany to stay with the Funcke family. My father came with me and stayed for a couple of days. Herr Funcke had died during the influenza epidemic in 1919, so Frau Funke brought up the children on her own. Their daughter, Christel, was one year older than I, her brother Paul was at university in Berlin and her younger brother Joachim was still at school and a member of the Hitler Youth. I remember having to say "Heil Hitler" to everybody, which I tried to avoid as much as possible. I was in

Germany from October 1938 to April 1939. The newspapers were full of how awful Britain was and running down Churchill. I was very annoyed by all this. The Funcke's were Nazis – Joachim was killed in the war, he was only 15 when I was there. To be a Nazi was quite normal and natural for people then. There was no war going on, everything had calmed down, we thought it was going to be all right.

1938 was exciting as thousands of young Jewish children were sent to England – three girls were taken into families in Crawley Down – all from Vienna. One of them asked me if I would mind bringing something back to England from her parents, still in Vienna, when she heard I was going to Hagen. So I, not having the vaguest idea, immediately said, "of course". Round about the time of my birthday a large parcel came for me from Vienna. I immediately thought, "ah-ha, this is the parcel from Hilda's parents". I had to make up a story to tell the Funcke's who wanted to know what was in it. I said I had friends

June skiing in the Dolomites

A Quadripartite FT Committee in the 1950's

A hiking trip

in Vienna and it was a birthday present. I took it upstairs to my room and opened it. Thank goodness I didn't open it in front of them! Inside was a red leather handbag stuffed full of jewellery. I hid everything as best I could and took the bag downstairs, and said "my friends sent me this lovely leather handbag". The problem was getting it out of the country – on leaving your luggage was always searched. I hid the jewellery in pots of cream and talcum powder tins – where I thought nobody could ever find it. The customs men came into the house to look at your luggage, but luckily they didn't really examine my trunk as the Funcke's were a well-known industrialist family.

Christel and I set off for England in April 1939, the plan being she would now come and stay in England for six months. My German had improved considerably and the Funcke's were very kind to me during my stay with them. My father met us at Victoria Station to accompany us to Crawley Down.

As the political situation worsened Christel's mother wrote saying she must come home. Christel left England at the beginning of August 1939. War broke out on the 6th September.

I was unsure of what I wanted to do. I knew I didn't want to go to university, I wasn't academically minded, so I thought I might do a secretarial course. Mrs Hoster's was supposed to be the second best

secretarial school in London, but they had been evacuated to Tunbridge Wells. This wasn't very far from where I was living having taken on a job as under matron at a school. I started the course in spring 1941. A month after starting the house was requisitioned and we moved to Grantham in Suffolk, to a mansion, where I completed my six-month course.

We had to learn typing with our gasmasks on – in case there was an air raid. I will always remember typing blind (you couldn't wear your glasses under the masks) to some American march music on the gramophone. It was an enjoyable time altogether. I learnt to type, take shorthand and German shorthand, committee procedure and all the kinds of things you would need if you obtained a good job. Mrs Hoster had an office in London, where you could then go for a month of work experience.

Mrs Hoster's aim was to obtain good jobs for her girls. First I had an interview with Lady Davidson, an MP in Parliament. A very nice person, she wanted me as a private secretary. However, I thought that wasn't such a good idea. I could still be called up as it wasn't an important war job, so I didn't take it. Then I saw an advertisement in the Daily Telegraph – people were wanted as secretaries to the Australian Air Force now quartered in London. I thought, having been born there, this was probably a good

idea. I travelled to London with my mother, because I, of course, was terrified. So I worked for the Australians, staying with Auntie Ruby at Elstree and travelling by tube every day. However, I didn't like it at all! Typing long lists of Air Force men coming over from Australia. It was awfully boring. I thought; "I'm not a typist".

I rang up Mrs Hoster and asked her help in finding me a new job. At that time a law was going to come into force decreeing if you didn't have a job or were about to change jobs you had to go and work in a factory. I desperately wanted to have a new job by the time this law was enforced. I received a letter asking "would I like to work at Downing Street and the Prime Minister's Office?"

"Yes, please!" I was interviewed by Miss Stenhouse, in the Annex, part of the Treasury Building. 10 Downing Street had been slightly bomb shaken and wasn't safe any longer.

I had to wait till the security checks were completed, to prove I wasn't spying for the Germans or anything like that. Finally I received the all clear and started work. I stayed with Lizzy Sealy, whom I later found out was working for MI5, but one wasn't allowed to know that. The shift system was 48 hours on duty and 48 hours off. I had to be there by 1:30pm, because it was safest to travel about then. I had to sign

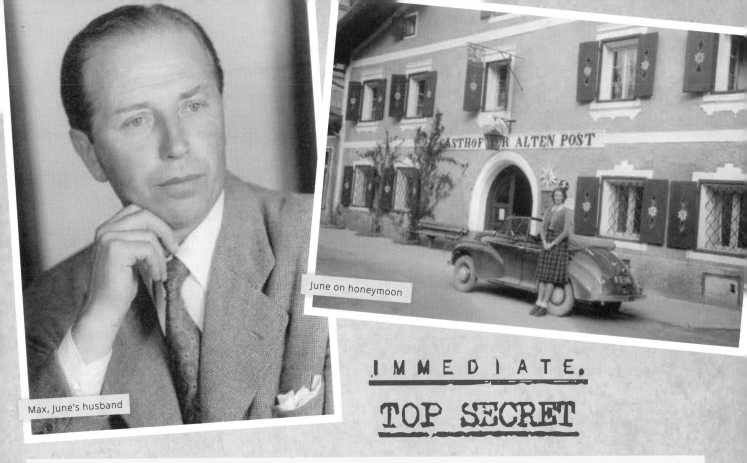

Max, June's husband

June on honeymoon

GASTHOF ZUR ALTEN POST

the Official Secrets Act before beginning work there – one was not allowed to write a diary or tell anybody at all what happened during the 48 hours at work. I stuck to the rules. I didn't write a diary – lots of people did judging by the books written afterwards.

We had sleeping quarters for the night during the shift. First we slept upstairs, on the same floor as our office. Then the bombing worsened and our sleeping quarters were moved into the depths. Our quarters had bunk beds, air-conditioning, and a telephone. The person on duty could be called at any time in the night to use the teleprinter, take shorthand, and carry out any necessary work. One private secretary always stayed till the Prime Minister went to bed, which was very late. Once when it was my turn to get up should anything

happen, the telephone rang. "The Prime Minister wishes to dictate". So, there I was in my dressing gown, going upstairs, in fear and trembling, because Churchill was a difficult man to cope with and hated to see new faces. I sat there in my dressing gown with my shorthand notebook waiting. The Prime Minister's bedroom was just next door. Then the message came through:

"The Prime Minister has gone to bed, nobody is needed". I don't think I could have coped, I wasn't terribly good at shorthand, and sometimes had difficulty in reading it.

One afternoon, when battles were being fought in Africa, Mr Rowan suddenly rang the bell: "come in, come in, there's a telegram that's very urgent, has to go to the PM straight away. It has to be dictated to you on the scrambler". Now the

scrambler was a special green telephone that scrambled messages so no spies could listen in. The dictation wasn't terribly clear. There was this man in the War Office dictating this telegram to me about the state of the battle in North Africa at great speed. I took it down as best I could, retreated into my office and sat down at the typewriter to type it down. But I couldn't read some of it; I was puzzling my brain, getting in an awful state. Mr Rowan kept coming in, "you've nearly finished?" The third time he came in, he said, "don't worry, scrap it. The telegram has already come over in the box from the War Office." My life was saved once more.

To reach the bathroom from our office, we had to walk through the Prime Minister's Annex, his private flat, across an outside corridor, past the stairs leading down to the War Cabinet. Once in the bathroom we were only allowed two inches of water and had to be very quick, so the next person could have their bath. One night after having my bath at the end of late duty I was going down to bed, two levels below the War Cabinet office. As I was walking down the stairs the War Cabinet door opened and they all came out, headed by the Prime Minister, followed by the Generals. There was I, pretending I didn't exist, standing in the corner of the staircase bend, pressed against the wall as they all marched past me. The last one to come up was General Smuts, the Prime Minister of South Africa, a very nice man. General Smuts obviously saw that I was very embarrassed by all this, so he stopped and said, "oh you are lucky, I wish I were you, I wish I could be going to bed too". That really was very kind of him. I was in my dressing gown made of two blue blankets; one couldn't buy material, except on coupons. It went down to the floor and buttoned up to the top, it was all quite decent.

I was at 10 Downing Street from the beginning of 1942 till the spring of '45. A memorandum had been circulating: "anybody wishing to join the British Element of the Austrian Commission going to be set up at the end of the war?" Everybody knew we were going to win the war, and everything was being organised beforehand for the Commissions for Germany and Austria. I thought it would be a cheap way of seeing Austria, so I put my name down. We were only temporary civil servants, meaning we wouldn't have a job after the war. I became the secretary of Rex Foy, the Head of the Trade and Supply Branch of the Economic Division.

As a farewell present I was given a silver topped oval glass trinket box engraved "10 Downing Street, 1942 – 1945". One had them on one's dressing table in those days and it was the done thing to give silver leaving presents. Having officially joined the Commission I had to be inoculated, medically examined, visit the organisation in Cromwell Road and be looked at, have my papers examined....it all took time. We were issued with uniforms and bedding – blankets and sheets. Therefore I was no longer at Downing Street when the war officially ended on the 8th May, which was a pity, as that would have been a great occasion. I received my "Movement Order" and my father accompanied me by train to Liverpool where I left on a troop ship from Liverpool docks on 10 May 1945. I was 24. The troop ship was blacked out in case there were any submarines still lurking about. On board there were officers and girls who were joining the Austrian Commission, mostly military with some civilians.

June's leaving letter from Downing Street

PRIME MINISTER

10, Downing Street,
Whitehall.

With every good wish

from

E. M. Watson.

September 1945 – June arrived in Austria after travelling through Italy.

1947 – The Commission was closing down and June's bags were packed to return home when Mr Daw, the first Commercial Counsellor in the Legation, offered her a job. While working there she met her future husband, Max. He was from Sudetenland, an architect and civil engineer. He was 13 years older than June and slightly shorter.

1950 – June and Max were married in Crawley Down. June had to leave the Legation because she was married to an Austrian and for security reasons could not remain there. Thus the Foreign Office transferred her to the Consulate as a locally engaged Austrian employee, where there was no risk of giving away any secrets! She lost her British passport because she was born in Australia and her father had been born in India. To receive a British passport again, she had to swear the Oath of Allegiance to the Queen. Thereafter she had a British and Austrian passport.

1951 – On the Saturday before Christmas, Max went to play chess with a friend. June was woken at 5 am by a policeman knocking at the door. Max had been involved in a bad car accident – his friend had been a fighter pilot in the war and was driving rather too fast on icy roads. The passenger in the back was killed, the driver had a broken nose and Max spent 3 years in hospital, his broken leg never fully recovered and he had to walk with a crutch.

18th March, 1958 – Max and June's daughter Stephanie was born. June had six weeks off work after the birth, followed by six weeks of sick leave. Then she was given an ultimatum – either go back to work or lose her job.

1968 – June first met the Queen and Prince Philip in Vienna

2nd January, 1979 – Max died.

29th July 1980 – June was awarded her Order of the British Empire at Buckingham Palace.

10th October 2010 at 10am – June slipped away peacefully and in quiet expectation of what she used to call "heaven"

"When June died I was living in Switzerland, though I had visited Vienna regularly and always took her out when I was there. I attended her memorial service held at Christ Church Vienna (where I was also married) on 12th November 2010. It was very touching having members of her family thank me for my work on putting together her life story, which they had thoroughly enjoyed reading. To the very end June always described herself as "very British"." - Sibylle

June's Wedding to Max

View of Red House from the front as approached from the street

THE RED *house*

Described by Edward Burne-Jones as "The beautifullest place on earth," *Nicole Burnett* meanders in awe around the iconic home of Arts and Crafts designer William Morris

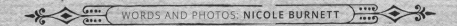

WORDS AND PHOTOS: NICOLE BURNETT

Life is short, but art endures – this Latin motto is inscribed over the drawing room fireplace of the only house William Morris built for himself. It has indeed become a lasting testament to his artistic and socialist ideals. The National Trust has owned it since 2003, and I was delighted to be invited along for a special tour and to meet its curator, Tessa Wild.

Visiting Red House in Bexleyheath, has been on my 'to do' list for the past 20 years ever since studying the Arts and Crafts movement at university. I have seen so many slides of this iconic building and often gazed at its aspects and interiors in the pages of books, so when I actually walked up the path towards the property for the first time

it felt surprisingly familiar; it was more like going to meet a personal hero than a house. For me, Red House symbolises passionate ideals made real. Or as we may say today, "putting your money where your mouth is to make your dreams come true!"

A backlash against industrialisation, sham design and the loss of traditional craft techniques had been brewing since the 1840s when the likes of John Ruskin and members of the Pre-Raphaelite Brotherhood started making a stand through their art and writings.

The young William Morris was hugely influenced by the Pre-Raphaelites, and whilst being educated at Oxford, from 1852, he met Edward Burne-Jones. He soon became fascinated with medievalism and socialist ideals, and

decided to dedicate his life to art.

In 1856 he started training as an architect and met Phillip Webb at the offices of G.E. Street. Webb was working as the chief assistant to Street, the great Gothic Revival architect and they became instant friends, sharing many of the same ideals. Morris' days as an architect were brief. However, Dante Gabriel Rossetti persuaded him to give it up to become a painter, so he set up a studio with friend Burne-Jones. While on their first commission with Rossetti at the Oxford Union debating chamber, they spotted the beautiful 17-year-old Jane Burden amongst the audience at the theatre, she became their main life-model and muse and Morris fell for her heavily.

The inspiration for Red House came during the summer of 1858 while Morris and Webb were on a touring holiday in France. (I can just imagine the young men getting totally carried away with ideas for its design and construction.)

Morris was by then engaged to Jane Burden and wanted to build a family home where they could live an idyllic life together. Webb was keen to help his friend and must have been aching to put his own unique architectural ideas into practice. Thanks to an inheritance from his father, William Morris could afford to buy land and build a house. He was passionate in his quest for good living and brave enough to take a risk and try something new. It was serendipity.

Without Red House, the Arts and Crafts movement may have remained just a puff of rose-tinted romanticism - it needed to be designed at precisely that time and, more importantly, to become a reality. The pressures of the real world could have taken hold of its idealists and like many rebels, they may eventually have been forced to conform (even if their souls remained true).

But Webb had the talent and a moneyed kindred spirit; the building of Red House became an important catalyst for both of them. It launched Webb's architectural career and, through his involvement with its furnishing, Morris was inspired to set up his own design firm in 1861; Morris, Marshall, Falkner and Co.. Red House helped to prove that the utopian ideals, which the emerging proteges of the Art and Crafts movement held dear at the time, were acceptable and even commercially viable and it rekindled an appreciation for craftsmanship and developed into an aesthetic style that would spread around the world.

The plans for Red House were complete by April 1859, when William married his "Janey", and a year later it was built at the cost of £4,000. It was never meant to be a showpiece or a tourist attraction but a home for family and friends, as Edward Burne-Jones said, it was "a house to be jolly in".

From the outside world it would

Red House as seen from the west

The pretty well with its witch's hat roof

The rose arbour over a red brick path

The recently planted kitchen garden to the north of the house

The front door painted with a zig-zag pattern

Stained-glass window with stylised birds designed by Philip Webb

blended into the landscape, an unpretentious masterpiece in red brick sitting in what was then, the Kent countryside, amongst orchards and oast houses. Today however, Red house is smack in the middle of 1930s suburbia and situated in Greater London. It is still surrounded by a substantial brick wall, hiding it from view and for me, walking through the gate to find a lovely country garden with one of the most famous houses in the world sitting in the middle of it was quite surreal.

Phillip Webb was an architect who excelled in practical design and common sense. The facade of Red House is dictated by its internal layout and function, making it charmingly random and unsymmetrical in appearance with an esoteric mix of windows of different shapes and sizes. Morris himself described the overall style as 13th century, but it is not at all pretentious, as Webb disliked pastiches of the past. Instead it is honest, makes good use of local materials and is inspired by humble barns and other ancient vernacular buildings.

I made the most of the sunshine and took a tour around the exterior. I wanted to take in every angle, to see which aspects I recognised from my studies. The most famous view is of the south side of the house with its bullseye windows and the pretty garden well with its witch's hat like clay-tiled roof.

The servants' quarters are on the north side of the house. They were spaciously designed and well thought out. Quality of life was considered carefully for all occupants of Red House. While they were living there the Morris' had four live-in servants; a cook, housemaid, nanny and groom.

Little remains of the original garden except for some old trees, but it is really delightful to walk around and it now has a enthusiastic gardener who has made a Victorian-style vegetable patch, and added a beehive. Combined with the aged brick paths, natural woodland planting, and rose archways, this ensures the garden complements the main house.

Door lintel detail in the entrance hall designed by Philip Webb

Detail of Burne-Jones stained glass window showing a figure of Fate

THE INTERIOR

Red House is now mostly empty, with only a few pieces of built-in furniture from Morris' time remaining, including a large settle-cum-cupboard in the hall, which is decorated with hand paintings by the artist, and a large medieval-style dresser in the dining room. Many of the original pieces are still in existence, displayed in museums or at Kelmscott Manor in Oxfordshire where William Morris moved in 1871.

It is fortunate that the various owners of Red House after Morris left were sympathetic to its style and appreciative of its architectural importance. Nevertheless it now looks very different to how it would have looked in its early years, with many of the walls and woodwork over-painted and its rooms decorated with William Morris wallpaper. In fact, Morris' wallpaper was never used in the house, as it had been sold before the designs were actually manufactured.

The National Trust have brought in select items in-keeping with the house, such as a Webb-designed table in the dining room, and they have been painstakingly stripping back the layers of white paint to reveal the original decorative schemes, which are startlingly colourful.

The decor of Red House was very much a joint effort between the Morris', the Burne-Jones' and their close circle of likeminded friends. They loved the idea of forming an artistic community, and at the weekends everyone came together to indulge in their love of pattern and design.

Morris disliked the modern taste in homeware, so instead he bought antiques and old pieces of metal-work, which he had collected in France. New items were made or designed by Morris or commissioned from friends. Edward Burne-Jones made some beautiful stained glass including the figure of Love, which can still be seen in the passageway.

Philip Webb designed dressers, tables, chairs, beds, copper candlesticks, table glass, grates

The upstairs drawing room, with inbuilt window seats and large dresser topped with a small minstrel's gallery

Original colourful medieval style paint scheme revealed from under the many layers of white paint

and even fire-irons especially for the house. Morris designed all the textiles at Red House; he had studied old embroidery techniques and taught Jane who was a talented needlewoman. She would work on embroidery frames with Georgiana Burne-Jones while the men sketched out designs on the walls.

To their fellow Victorians, this form of interior design must have been viewed as quite shocking, in much the same way as we view graffiti art today. However, the freedom of expression and hands-on style must have seemed very liberating to those contributing to the house's decoration. There was no pretence, no rules to follow, they treated the rooms as blank canvases and let their

Red brick fireplace from the drawing room, one of many designed for the house by Philip Webb

Detail of one of the few surviving wall murals - this one in the drawing room showing The Marriage Procession of Sir Degrevant

A reconstruction of some of the many original wall decoration designs at Red House

Morris and Co designed wallpaper - was added to various rooms in the house during the 20th century, but were not used during the Morris familiy's time

The spectacular painted ceiling in the stairwell - the design looks much more modern than its 1860 date

Fireplace with Delft tiles chosen by William Morris

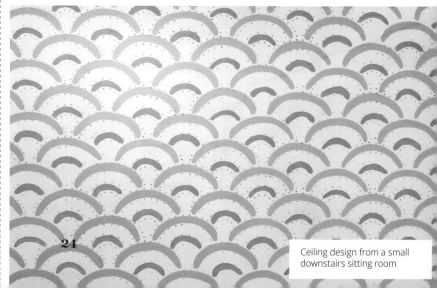

24

Ceiling design from a small downstairs sitting room

imaginations run wild inspired by medieval folklore and classical tales.

My favourite room is the upstairs drawing room and despite its rather stark appearance today, underneath the white paint glimpses of a lavish jewel like medieval palette have been revealed not only on the walls, but on the ceiling and woodwork too. The original settle remains, along with fragile pieces of glorious wall murals. Burne-Jones was commissioned to paint seven around the room based on the medieval romance of Sir Degrevant. Sadly, only three were completed, The Wedding, The Wedding Procession and The Wedding Feast. The bride and groom in the final scene are in fact portraits of William and Jane.

Many of the ceilings in the house were decorated in bold geometric patterns, and the most spectacular is the one at the top of the staircase; the pattern was marked out in

The wooden stairway; simple design showing its construction with French medieval style turrets and small holes cut in the side panels to frame interesting views

Embroidery panel sewn by Jane Morris and her sister-in-law showing Aphrodite. Intended as one of 12, based on a Chaucer poem for the dining room

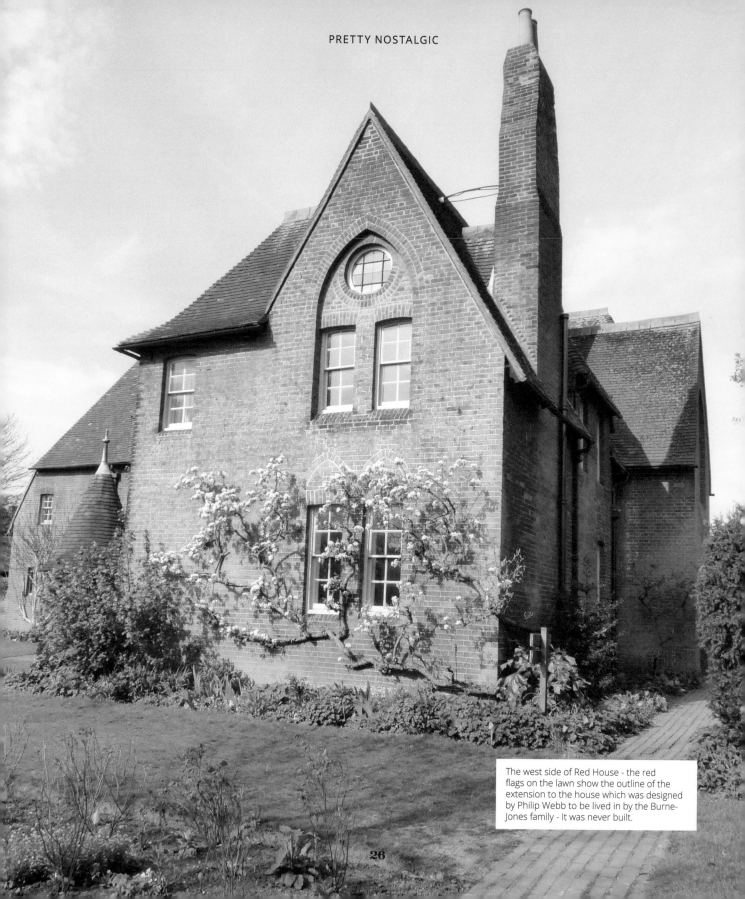

The west side of Red House - the red flags on the lawn show the outline of the extension to the house which was designed by Philip Webb to be lived in by the Burne-Jones family - It was never built.

the plasterwork by making a series of little holes and these would have been drawn in like a large dot-to-dot. Surprisingly, they look more like Art Deco or even modernist rather that Arts and Crafts.

THE END OF AN ERA

It seems that the early years of enthusiastic decorating didn't last very long and many of the rooms were uncompleted. The arrival of the Morris children, Jenny in 1861 and May in 1862 and the increasing pressures of Morris' new business took their toll. They adored life at Red House and there was a plan to move the business out to Bexleyheath, and for the Burne-Jones family who loved the house equally to move into their own wing, which Phillip Webb had been commissioned to design, but it was not meant to be.

The Morris family left the Red House in 1865 after living in it only five years. The realities of life had eventually caught up with them. Georgiana Burne-Jones had lost a child, both William and Jane were unwell and their marriage was rocky. To make things worse Morris' annual income from his father's inheritance had fallen sharply and the constant travelling to and from London to tend to the ever-more demanding furnishing business was taking its toll. The bubble had burst. It was said to be more than Morris could bear, but again it may have been a heartache which needed to happen, and the loss of Red House may have been as much a catalyst as its building. The Arts and Crafts Movement had been set in motion and William Morris was to become one of the greatest designers, writers and social reformers of the 19th century.

VISITING RED HOUSE

Red House is owned by the National Trust and members can visit for free.

To check opening days and times visit nationaltrust.org.uk/red-house There is a café, shop and second-hand book shop on site and lots of activities for children and adults scheduled regularly.

**Red House Lane,
Bexleyheath,
London,
DA6 8JF
020 8304 9878
redhouse@nationaltrust.org.uk**

Duck stained glass designed by Philip Webb.

A–Z OF *Sylko Threads*

A ASTRAL GOLD
Just one of the several shades of gold that was available, proving just how diverse the choice of Sylko threads was. Other golds included Old Gold, Honey Gold and Mustard Gold.

B *Buckingham Lilac.*
One of my favourites, this is a delightfully foppish name and colour. It makes me think of Great Aunts using it to monogram their lacy hankies.

C CHINESE GREEN
Although many of the colour names used British themed descriptors, a few were given a more exotic title. Monaco Blue, Morocco Red and Firenze Blue are other examples of this colour genre.

D UCK EGG BLUE
Surely a million baby boys' matinee jackets had their buttons sewn on with this colour thread.

E EAU DE NIL
This is a beautiful pale green/blue. The old fashioned name translates as 'Water of the Nile'. I've never been to Africa but I feel sure that the Nile hasn't been this colour in a long time!

F *Festive Orange*
This is a vivid Jaffa coloured thread - it is the colour of an orange in your stocking on Christmas morning.

G GAY KINGFISHER
This name ranks high on everyone's list of favourites! It is a reminder that when these colours were named, the word gay had a wholly different meaning to today's usage.

H HORTICULTURAL COLOURS
Many colours were named after our favourite flowers and plants - the garden was perhaps the most common colour reference point. Examples include Gladiole Red, Forget-Me-Not and Peach Rose.

I *Indian Curry*
I think that this must have been a 1970s colour innovation...trying to prove that Sylko colours were keeping up with the times!

J JEWEL COLOURS
These colours are still very attractive and highly desirable to modern eyes – Sapphire, Amethyst or Emerald are all ideal for jazzing up your cushion edgings or sewing on sequins.

K KHAKI
At least three shades of khaki were produced, a product of a world which saw frequent wars and National Service. Thousands of army buttons must have been sewn on with khaki Sylko.

L *Lime Tint*
I've been using this one a lot lately when stitching pieces of vintage map. This colour blends perfectly with the green areas on Bartholomew cloth maps.

M — Moss Green

Moss Green I would categorise this one as part of the Sylko natural history collection – earthy camouflage colours. Others include Grass Green, Bracken and Slate.

N — NUTMEG

NUTMEG Part of the herb and spice names category. Others include Sage, Cinnamon Brown, and Saffron.

R — ROSE DU BARRI

ROSE DU BARRI Named after a ceramic glaze colour; a rather unusual source for a Sylko colour name. It reminds me of flamboyant Edwardian ladies with feathers in their hats.

U — UNPUNCTURED LABEL

UNPUNCTURED LABEL *When a Sylko reel was used on a sewing machine, the label on each end of the reel inevitably became punctured. Those reels that escaped this and have their labels in tact are more desirable today.*

V — VERY DARK PEACOCK

VERY DARK PEACOCK The use of the term 'very dark' is something of a cop-out in naming terms, I feel! Perhaps the usual colour naming person (I wish I knew who this was) was on holiday that day.

X — X-RATED

X-RATED Unfortunately there is one colour name that cannot be printed here. This is indicative of the casual racism of the earlier 20th Century, and demonstrates how far we have moved on in our attitudes to people of other nationalities.

O — One Hundred Yards

One Hundred Yards *The length of cotton on a standard reel, as stated on the iconic label.*

S — Solent

Solent I've not counted, but I'm sure that blue is the Sylko colour with the most variations. There is a positive plethora of blues available, but I particularly like this colour name as it plays on the British love for our naval heritage.

JOHN DEWHURST & SONS
BELLE VUE MILLS SKIPTON

W — WOODEN VERSUS PLASTIC

WOODEN VERSUS PLASTIC *The plastic reels took over from wooden ones sometime in the late 1960s or early 1970s. All vintage lovers will agree that the wooden bobbins are much more evocative. They give the holder much more of a sense of history within the tactile weight of the wood.*

Y — YORKSHIRE

YORKSHIRE I am proud that Sylko cotton was made in my home county for most of its life. The thread was made at Dewhurst's Belle Vue Mills in Skipton until closure in 1983.

P — PARMA VIOLET

PARMA VIOLET This is the most beautifully vivid purple. It reminds me of a foil chocolate wrapper, which is perhaps why I am so drawn to it!

Q — Quantity

Quantity Colours were numbered, and the numbers top 500, demonstrating again the sheer breadth of shades available.

T — TURKEY RED SHADE

TURKEY RED SHADE *This is a rather unusual colour name in that it uses the word 'shade' – which I have not seen on any other colour. It is a vivid red, but the question is – is it named after the bird's neck or the Turkish flag?*

Z — ZERO

ZERO *The colours of black and white were not allocated numbers – they were too ubiquitous to need one! The world was a much more monochrome place until relatively recently.*

WORDS: SARAH MILLER WALTERS

STUCK ON
shoe

Mixed Media artist **Gabriela Szulman** shows us how to turn boring boots into spectacular footwear, with just paper and glue!

WORDS AND PHOTOS: **GABRIELA SZULMAN**

The layering of found imagery and memorabilia runs across all my creations, whether they are mixed media works on canvas, paper collages, printed designs for my scarf or jewellery collections, or decoupaged objects. I have a growing archive of vintage magazines, scraps of paper, postcards, letters and photographs that provide me with reference material and inspiration. I am also drawn to colour and pattern, both of which are strong elements in my work.

My interest in decoupage took off some 18 months ago in a big way. A few facts about decoupage: the word comes from the French découper – meaning to cut out- and the practice arose in the late 17th century as a cheap way to copy the look of intricately painted Venetian furniture. In the 18th century, the craft became such a rage among upper-class French women that they cut up paintings by noted artists such as Watteau and Fragonard for their decoupage projects. In the 21st century, however, it is less widely used, maybe due to

its rather naff association with glossy knick-knacks featuring far too many flowers, but has been adopted and adapted by artists.

My take on this versatile technique has been to explore it and develop innovative ways of incorporating it into what I make. But let me go back to my decoupage "turning point" now: it happened when one of my sisters taught me how to upcycle a pair of old boots with just paper and glue. Soon I was hooked and I moved to trays, picture frames, chairs, old suitcases, which I use to display my work.

I experimented with lots of different papers and found that the results I liked best were those achieved using very thin printed tissue or paper napkins: a laborious process which is well worth the time and patience involved. Of course I now have another treasure trove: beautiful printed papers from a variety of sources that I pick up anywhere from supermarkets to art shops, to use in my work and also to share with those who attend my decoupage and mixed media workshops.

WHY DECOUPAGE SHOES?

By now you may be thinking this may not be the brightest idea given we live in a notoriously rainy country. As a committed fan of decoupage shoes I'm going to try to convert you! Here are my reasons:

- They are such a fun thing to do: a project you can complete in an afternoon, even better when done with a group of friends and a supply of tea and cake.
- It's a great way to upcycle shoes you may not wear any more, or perhaps a pair you've found in a charity shop that fit perfectly but are the wrong colour.
- You'll end up with something unique: your very own piece of "wearable art".
- As long as it's not pouring down with rain, you'll be able to wear your decoupage shoes indoors and out: treat them as you would fabric or suede shoes.
- They will last you a couple of years in good condition, and after that you can decoupage them again!

HERE IS WHAT YOU'LL NEED TO
DECOUPAGE A PAIR OF SHOES:

TOOLS AND MATERIALS

- A couple of medium-size flat paint
  brushes, an old kabuki or shaving brush
- Scalpel, nail scissors
- Paper towels, soft cloth, newspaper
- White acrylic paint or acrylic primer
- Sanding block, fine grade sanding paper
- Patterned paper napkins
- Glue – I recommend "Mod Podge
  outdoor" for this project. Alternatively,
  you could use normal Mod Podge
  decoupage glue and then seal with the
  outdoor version.

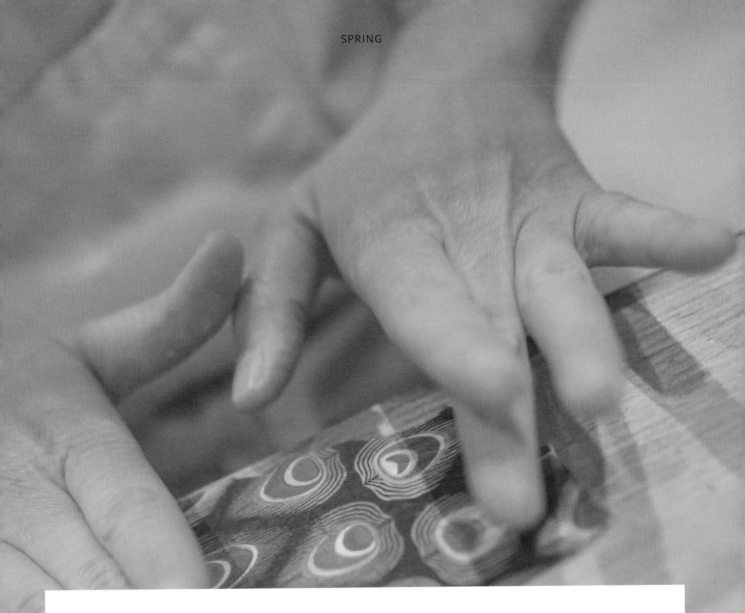

PROCESS:

1. Find an old pair of shoes – leather or plastic work best, avoid suede or fabric. Patent leather may need light sanding down to provide a "key" for the paint but otherwise is fine. The heel and sole should be sound – if not, I suggest you get them repaired beforehand. The plainer the shoes, the easier they will be to decoupage. If they have any pleats, studs, embroidery or other embellishments you may need to work around those.

2. Cover your table with newspaper and then proceed to clean either the whole shoe or just the area you intend to decoupage with a piece of cloth soaked in methylated spirits. The purpose of this is to remove old polish, dirt and /or anything greasy that may be on the surface of the shoe.

3. If the shoes are dark (black, brown, navy blue) it is best to give them a coat of white acrylic

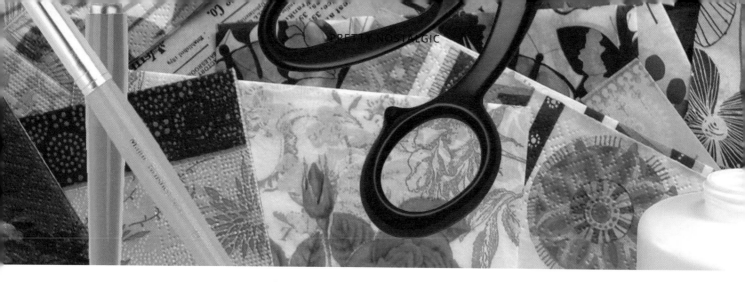

primer or acrylic paint first, as napkin paper is very transparent and therefore looks best on a light background. If in doubt, test your paper first: paint half a square of white card with black acrylic and then glue the paper across both halves to see how it looks on dark vs light background.

4. Wait for the paint to dry – 20 to 30 minutes depending on the atmosphere. Use a hairdryer on warm setting if feeling impatient.

5. If the shoes are very soft and pliable, you may find it helpful to stuff the front with newspaper or cloth.

6. Prepare the paper - napkins have three layers: you want to separate them and keep just the top one. Use the tip of a scalpel knife if you find it difficult to peel the layers: the way to tell you've got the top layer only is that it will be very thin and fragile.

7. Decide on your pattern - random torn pieces work best and are easiest to apply. It is possible to glue a

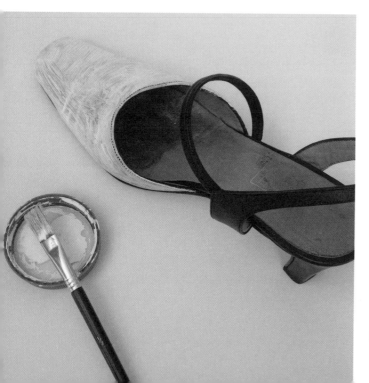

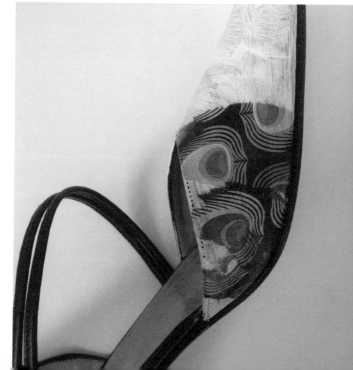

larger pattern in place once you've had practice but I suggest you work small initially.

8. Starting from the border of the shoe, paint a very thin layer of glue, pat down a piece of paper with your finger and lightly brush a watered-down layer of glue on top. Do the same with the next piece, slightly overlapping on the previous one. Alternate between shoes if the surface starts getting soggy. Avoid touching the pieces of paper you've just glued as you may lift them. Once the whole area is covered, allow to dry.

9. When the shoes are completely dry, trim any untidy edges with the scalpel. Then sand down any uneven or wrinkled areas with the sanding block – do this very lightly as otherwise you may tear the paper. Dust the powder off with the kabuki or shaving brush.

10. Paint a thin layer of glue all over. Allow to dry: you may notice that this top layer stays tacky for quite a while, as it takes 2-3 days for it to "cure" and dry completely. After that your upcycled shoes are ready to wear and be admired!

Needles at the ready!

Take part in our Nostalgianeer Needlework Challenge!

"Needlework has been a means of taking a woman out of herself, and has been quite a refuge from her troubles and anxieties, and the fact of seeing her work growing prettier and better has been a pleasure."

Needlework is an ancient art and has always been a pleasurable hobby, originally decorative stitch work was the reserve of ladies with the financial means and the leisure time to indulge. Working class women usually had so much general making and mending to do that there was little time left for more artistic pursuits. However, in the 1920s and 30s embroidery in particular was taken up in earnest by all classes.

There were a few factors which helped it reach mass popularity; on a practical level the introduction of electric lighting into homes meant women were able to see enough to stitch throughout the winter months when there was little else to do during the dark nights. Also, stitching was something productive and could be done while listening to the radio. Many women would have felt they were frivolous with their time if they just sat and listened.

It was the women's magazines of the 1920s to 1950s, that particularly popularised the fashion for embroidery; transfer patterns were a cheap, free gift given out to readers in order to encourage sales. They were also an easy way to capitalise on womens' innate desire to create beautiful and useful items for their home, especially when they had more time than money available to them. Every woman was encouraged to make items of decorated linen for their bottom drawer even before meeting a suitable husband and talented needlewomen could ensure they stood out from the crowd by embellishing their clothing, collars, cuffs, belts and bags with colourful designs, often incorporating sequins and beads. These embroidered articles would have been proudly displayed, carefully used and treasured, and in old age they would have been looked upon fondly as a reminder of youthful nimble fingers and memories of setting up home.

Of course needlework is still enjoyed by many today, but it is not as widespread as it once was. It is true that we have many more options for evening distractions, but perhaps many of us have never been introduced to embroidery before, don't feel we would be any good at it, simply afraid to give it ago.

So, this is the first of our Pretty Nostalgic Nostalgianeer Challenges – we will set our members new challenges each compendium. This time, we would like you to have a go at some vintage-style hand embroidery. On the following pages you will find some lovely designs taken from original 1930s patterns, instructions on how to transfer them onto your chosen fabric and also some illustrations of popular vintage stitches. We will provide further instructions, tutorials on the member pages of our website (**prettynostalgic.co.uk**) and we would love you to let us know how you get on and send us photos of your efforts which we will share.

This is your chance to have a go at something new or to show us how accomplished you already are. By working together and sharing knowledge, experience and advice who knows what we can achieve over the coming years?

"How delightful it is to be able to make pretty and decorative things for our homes! There is far more pleasure in being able to say 'Yes, I worked that,' instead of 'I bought it at such and such a shop'. We should not depend wholly on the work of others sold in the shops for the beautifying of our houses, or our rooms or even our own persons." Art Needlework c1920

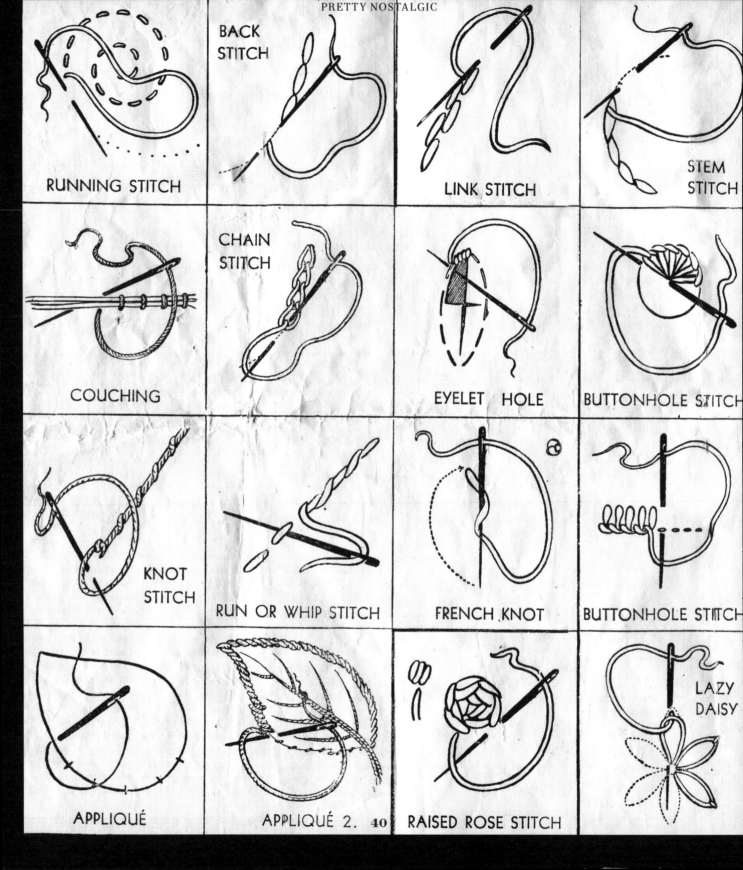

RUNNING STITCH

BACK STITCH

LINK STITCH

STEM STITCH

COUCHING

CHAIN STITCH

EYELET HOLE

BUTTONHOLE STITCH

KNOT STITCH

RUN OR WHIP STITCH

FRENCH KNOT

BUTTONHOLE STITCH

APPLIQUÉ

APPLIQUÉ 2. 40

RAISED ROSE STITCH

LAZY DAISY

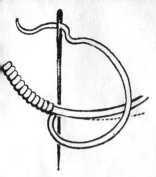

OVERCAST STITCH

STRAIGHT STITCH

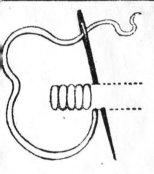

SATIN STITCH

SINGLE STITCHES

Embroidery Advice

Choosing your project

Decide what you would like to decorate with your embroidery. Don't start anything too difficult or you are in danger of losing interest and giving up before you see the results. A handkerchief or a plain scrap of linen, which you can use as a patch or even frame afterwards, will give you an easy first project, but of course feel free to be adventurous and as creative as you like. Wash and iron your fabric before use.

Transferring the pattern

Print out the following pages of transfer patterns and choose which one you would like to embroider. There are various ways you can transfer the pattern, but whichever method you use make sure the pattern once transferred is the right way around and not back to front. If you are artistic you may be able to copy the pattern free hand onto your fabric with a soft pencil.

Dressmaker's carbon paper

Place the carbon paper gently over the spot you wish to embroider then place the pattern on top and lightly pin the corners in place. Gently trace over every line of the pattern using a pencil or a knitting needle, using enough pressure for the carbon to transfer its ink onto the fabric clearly.

Transfer pens or pencil

Both transfer pens and pencils allow you to trace over the photocopied pattern and then you can turn it over and iron the transfer pattern to your fabric.

Needle and threads

Embroidery thread is also called floss and is sold in skeins. There are a huge number of colours to choose from, but start with just a few contrasting colours. The thread is multi strand and the most common have six strands, for simple stitches just use one strand of thread, but if you want thicker stitches you can use two threads at a time. After threading your needle make a knot at the end and then trim off the excess. Use a crewelwork needle, the sharp point and large eye make them easy to work with. They come in sizes 1-10 with size 1 having the smallest eye. Beginners are best to starting with a size 7-10 which can take a doubled thread easily.

Final advice

Do a few test stitches on some scrap fabric first and then make a start on your pattern, if you make a mistake you can always unpick. Work one colour at a time and try not to travel too far between stitches or the back will be messy and you will get your threads into a tangle. You can use an embroidery frame to keep the fabric tight and easy to manage, but for most small patterns you should be able to manage without one.

Further help and advice can be found on our website. Don't forget to show us your final results! Share photos of your embroidery online or by emailing **hello@prettynostalgic.co.uk**.

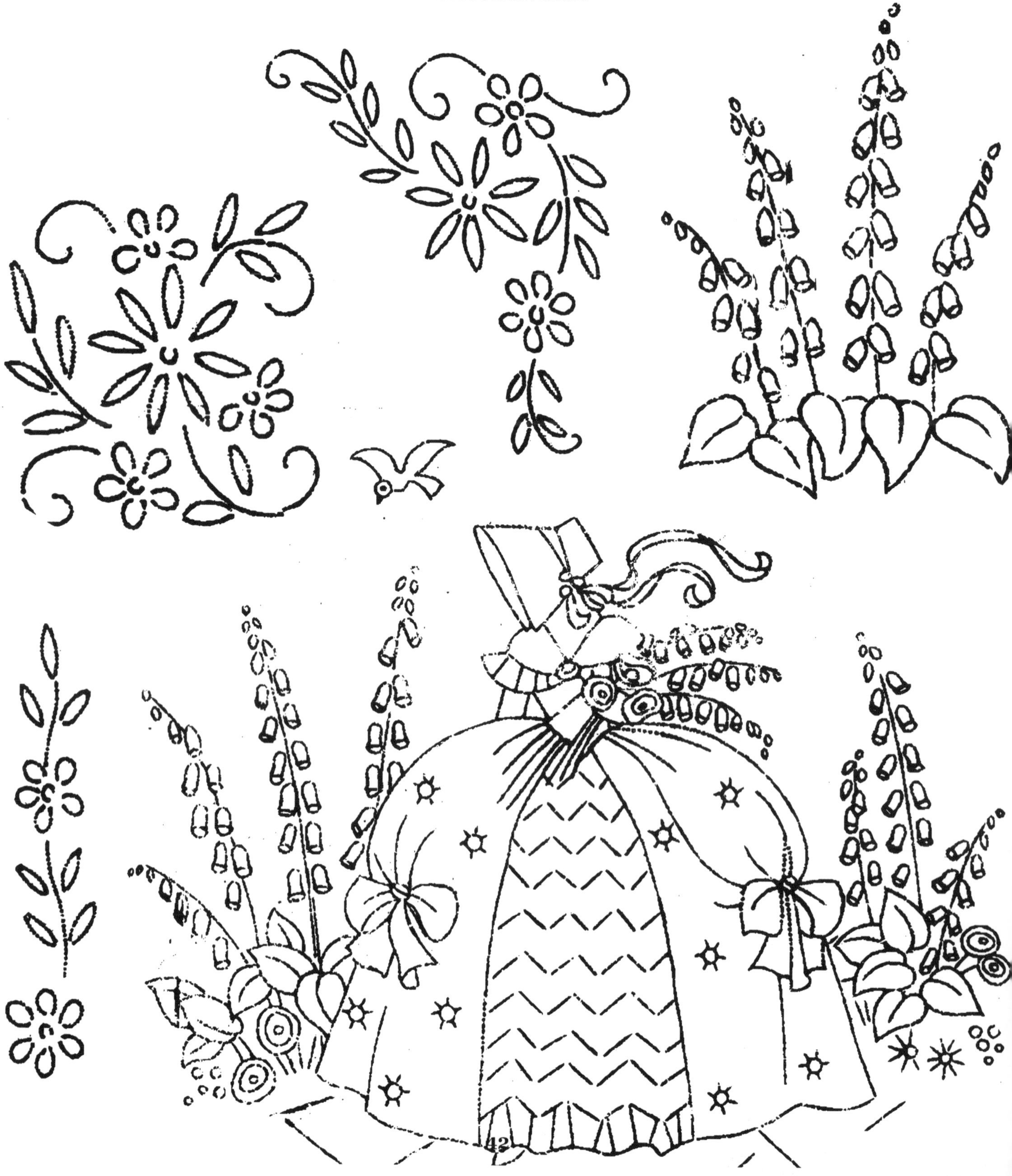

GRIFFIN *towers*

We take an around the world tour in the Clevedon home of two dedicated Nostalgianeers

WORDS: **NICOLE BURNETT**

I met Paul and Denny Welcomme last year, and I could instantly tell they were Pretty Nostalgic people; after a quick chat and a flick through our back issues, they signed up as members straightaway and later committed to becoming lifetime members when we ran our Kickstarter campaign. I was keen to get to know them better, and knew that if their house reflected our shared interests as much as I thought, then it would certainly be worth showing to our readers.

I wasn't wrong, Paul and Denny have been true Nostalgianeers all their lives and their modest Victorian villa in the seaside town of Clevedon is a virtual telephone exchange to the past. There are connections to people, places and events woven through every single item

they own, sparking memories and interesting stories at every turn.

Denny, who trained in fashion and textiles, has a real passion for Victoriana, and bought the house, affectionately called Griffin Towers after its street name, in the early 1990s. Paul joined her 10 years ago after they met at a friend's Handfasting in Ireland. The house dates from 1883 and is part of a terrace built to accommodate the increase in travellers arriving at the nearby Clevedon railway station, providing bed and breakfast and laundry services.

"It had been empty for a year and was considered uninhabitable when I bought it," explains Denny. "The kitchen was in the 'lean-to' at the back under a

corrugated plastic roof and the windows were boarded up. It needed re-wiring and a new roof and don't even mention the damp, but the atmosphere just grabbed me. It was a family house just waiting to be loved."

COME INTO THE PARLOUR

The living room has a very Victorian parlour feel about it with heavy carved oak furniture, lots of interesting knick-knacks and comfy armchairs arranged for conversations around the fire, rather than watching television. The fireplace however, has caused a conflict of conscience for Denny over the years. "I've had a love/hate relationship with the fireplace," she confesses. "Its 1930s 'Odeon' design clashes with the style I wanted for the house, however it is quite a spectacular feature and I've grown to appreciate it over time. I doubt it would survive removal and I can't bear the thought of it being broken up."

It is this reaction which marks Denny out as

a true Nostalgianeer: Someone decorating in a 'vintage style' would have thoughtlessly ripped it out and replaced it with one to fit the look they wanted (even horror of horrors, with a mass produced copy!) however, Nostalgianeers look at objects with feeling and emotion and these will often outweigh aesthetics, leaving interiors which are heartfelt and quirky, and impossible to fake.

Most of the furniture in the house is inherited, including the Norfolk oak dresser in the living room which came from Paul's father after he died in 2013. They especially like the Green Man on the carved doors and this motif appears many times around the house and in the garden.

Paul appreciates all the furniture and the objects they have collected. "We both love the feeling of being at home, a cosy and comfortable place to rest, work and play alongside things we have found, bought, inherited, polished and cared for, and too many old books."

On the wall of the living room there is a striking portrait of a Vietnamese girl, painted by Paul's father who was inspired by a newspaper photo during the Vietnam War. "My father developed his artistic skills as an engineering apprentice before the war," says Paul. "He then entered the RAF and in the late 1960s he was posted to Cyprus as a Wing Commander and he took up oil painting as a 'siesta time' hobby. I have inherited several of his paintings and this is my favourite. My father continued painting into his 90s and amazingly he was red/green colour blind so had to check often with my mother that he hadn't painted the wrong colour sky!"

FAR FLUNG PLACES

As you move around the house, it's a bit like partaking in a Grand Tour of British colonial history, with fascinating objects from Africa, India and other far flung places springing into view at every angle. Denny has always been drawn to India: "My Dad was there during the war and my grandfather was born there, in Madras I believe. On their last trip together they brought back two colourful wall hangings

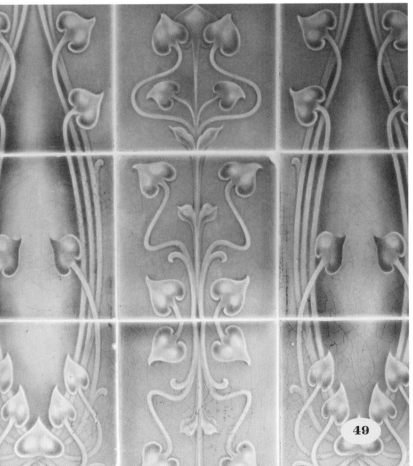

and a hand-loomed silk duvet." As for Paul, he feels an affinity with the colour and vibrancy of Africa, partly inspired by watching David Attenborough and also hearing stories from his uncle, Professor Robin Welcomme who was a renowned marine biologist working in east Africa. "In my mid-forties, I fell in love with the rhythmic music of Africa and learned to play the djenmbe and in 2003 I did a fundraising climb of Kilimanjaro in Tanzania".

The hallway displays wall hangings bought on a trip to Bolivia and Peru as well as a small gallery of historical views of Clevedon, where they are both very happy living, describing it as a "lovely Victorian built town by the sea with a beautifully restored pier, but still small enough for people in the nearby shops to remember your name." They are both actively involved in the local transition group and help to raise awareness of energy consumption and recycling.

The dining room has even more of a Victorian feel and here Denny has managed to restore a period fireplace and above it sits one of her favourite pieces, an old model of a ship in its original case which was rescued after a long hibernation in her father's garage (he would have been a strong Nostalgianeer but his wife's view was disapproving hence it being in the garage!). "I like things to show signs of age, not to be too perfect – not spoilt by being overly 'tarted up', just like Paul," she says with a laugh. The dining room also holds two of Paul's favourite items; Robbie the roebuck which was given to them as a wedding present in 2013 and also a leather-sheathed Kukri Knife which was given to his father by his Indian colleagues when he served in Ceylon.

CUPBOARD LOVE

Towards the back of the house, the area which would have been the original kitchen is now a pretty breakfast room and the kitchen has been installed into a more substantial extension to the side. Both Paul and Denny spent over a year poring over magazines looking for the perfect kitchen and in the end they designed it

themselves and found a company in Bristol to make it to their specifications. They re-installed the original Belfast sink which was being used as a plant container in the garden and the large deep cupboards were inspired by the Victorian kitchens of nearby National Trust house, Tyntesfield, where Denny had worked as an inventory volunteer. "We smile every time we walk into our lovely kitchen" they both say, beaming. Even in the kitchen there are inherited antiques like Denny's Nanna's sturdy iron saucepans which sit happily on a bottom shelf, and reclaimed items mix nicely with the new. Paul points to the cooker. "The green Victorian kitchen tiles we found at an antique and collectable sale we stumbled across on our travels, I think it was on the way to Stamford, Lincolnshire. They obviously came from a fireplace but we managed to make the pattern work as a block of nine so that the pattern looks like heat rising".

Upstairs there are two double bedrooms and a large bathroom overlooking the garden, which has practical timber cladding painted an attractive dark green and a useful Victorian airer hoisted over a lovely old-fashioned radiator. A small laundry room next door displays vintage washing powder packaging, rescued from Denny's brother's house.

The Welcomme's home is quite literally a live-in memory box, which is not only special to them but fascinating for visitors too. They try to encompass every aspect of their life into it, even down to the railway memorabilia, which has crept in since Denny started working for Great Western Railways. It is clear they have been embracing the Pretty Nostalgic ethos of 'Spend Wisely, Waste Less and Appreciate More' quite naturally. I felt very proud to see our Pledge calendar displayed on the side of their china cupboard when I walked through their house and I am very honoured to have them both as lifelong members of Pretty Nostalgic too.

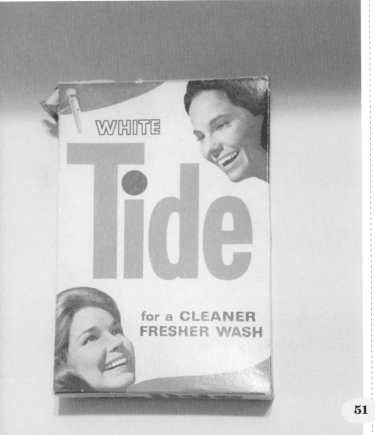

THE HOUSE
beautiful

THE WINDOW SEAT

A window seat is a beautiful edition to any home; it is the classic refuge for daydreamers and those seeking sanctuary from the pressures of everyday life. They are the perfect place to read a favourite book, especially if tucked away behind the curtains and their access to natural daylight makes them a wonderful location for sewing or knitting.

I want to share with you some delightful period window seats found in the Pretty Nostalgic Archives, the first, which we have also used on the cover, dates from 1883 and is taken from one of the most enchanting Victorian children's book called at Home Again by Thomas Crane and J. G Sowerby, both famous Aesthetic designers.

The other window seats are taken from an early 20th century home furnishing catalogue for Williamson and Cole Ltd, who had showrooms in Clapham in London. The illustrations date from around 1918 and this catalogue is a rare survival, there are few colour images of furnishing schemes from this time and the sumptuous colours and patterns are just wonderful. I hope you enjoy looking at them and that they may inspire you to install a window seat in your own home.

"A window-seat, which look's well over the front of the home, and yet does not serve as a "Gazaboo" as some old country folk call an old maid's window over looking the doing of her neighbours."

A GENTLEWOMAN'S HOME – A DREAM HOUSE 1896
MRS J E PANTON

WRITE FOR
PATTERNS

PATTERNS
POST FREE.

HAVANA.
SPRING

RED.
ROSE.

WATERCRESS.
JADE.

CANARY.
TANGERINE.

SAPPHIRE.
LILAC.

SUGGESTION S.P.

"SUNWIN" NANKIN

MAUVE
Guaranteed Unfadable.

30 inches wide.

ROSE

..en, Brown, Rose, Tussore, Gobelin, Wine.
DELFT.
Guaranteed Unfadable.

55

A Decorative Window Treatment of "SUNPRUF" Fabrics

"The window seat provides a very pleasing addition to a small sitting-room, both from an artistic and a utilitarian point of view.... The framework of the seat is very simple, but neat and strong. If liked, the front could be boxed in, thus forming a useful and capacious receptacle for holding needlework, books, toys etc.

CASSELLS HOUSEHOLD GUIDE 1912

A TASTE OF
INDIA

Our perception today is that a good British curry is a modern creation – but is that really the case? *Nicole Burnett* finds out.

WORDS AND PHOTOS: **Nicole Burnett**

I count myself as a very British person and I love great British food, but for as long as I can remember, my "go to" food for special occasions and as a treat has been a curry. I don't think I am alone in this and perhaps my love of a good curry is a signifier of how British I really am, what with chicken tikka masala supposedly our nations' favourite dish.

I remember as a small child begging my parents for a taste of their rare home cooked curries, this was the 1970s so it was a "Homepride Cooking Sauce" - out of a tin, but its smell was irresistible to me as it wafted through the house when I should have been fast asleep. My mother would give in and as I sat in my dressing gown dipping morsels of sliced white bread into a small bowl of the aromatic brown liquor, which hid the occasional exotic sultana or chunk of pineapple, my tongue would tingle with the spicy heat and I would relish every mouthful, hoping that soon I would be able to share the feast for real. It was a good few years before I was seen as old enough to partake in a real Indian takeaway on a Saturday night and I would never have been taken out for an Indian meal, which is a treat my children have enjoyed since birth.

The Brits have been enraptured by the complex taste of a good curry for hundreds of years, ever since the first members of the East India Company started trading spices with Indian merchants at the start of the 17th century. The word curry is thought to be an adopted anglicised term, taken from the Tamil word Kari meaning a "sauce". Hannah Glasse in her famous book *The Art of Cookery* made plain and easy, which was first published in 1747, seems to have written the first British recipe for curry.

By reading the ingredients, it doesn't appeal as a recipe I would want to recreate, with the only spices used being black pepper and coriander seeds, it seems very unlikely that this would taste much like a curry we would think of today. Of course it is impossible to tell whether this was a true Indian recipe or a concoction made up to appease the curious taste buds of the many Georgians who were unable to access the real thing. It is true, however, that the use of chillies and very hot spices was not as common in India as it is today, but certainly a larger combination of spices would have flavoured the dishes than Hannah Glasse portrayed.

TO MAKE A CURRY
THE INDIA WAY

"Take two fowls or rabbits, cut them into small pieces, and three or four small onions, peeled and cut very small, thirty Pepper Corns, and a large Spoonful of Rice, Brown some coriander Seeds over the Fire in a clear Shovel, and bear them to a Powder, take a Tea Spoonful of Salt, and mix all well together with the Meat, put all together into a sauce-pan or stew-pan, with a Pint of Water, let it stew softly till the meat is tender enough, then put in a piece of fresh Butter, about as big as a large Walnut, shake it well together, and when it is smooth and fine Thickness, dish up, and send it to the Table; if the Sauce be too thick, add a little more Water before it is done, and more Salt if it wants it. You are to observe the Sauce must be pretty thick."

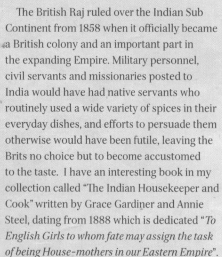

The British Raj ruled over the Indian Sub Continent from 1858 when it officially became a British colony and an important part in the expanding Empire. Military personnel, civil servants and missionaries posted to India would have had native servants who routinely used a wide variety of spices in their everyday dishes, and efforts to persuade them otherwise would have been futile, leaving the Brits no choice but to become accustomed to the taste. I have an interesting book in my collection called "The Indian Housekeeper and Cook" written by Grace Gardiner and Annie Steel, dating from 1888 which is dedicated "*To English Girls to whom fate may assign the task of being House-mothers in our Eastern Empire*".

The pages are filled with advice on how to manage a household in different regions of India and how to deal with the local staff. The recipes it contains are mostly very English, perhaps in the vain hope that their staff could be taught how to make some of their favourite meals from home. Very few Indian dishes were included and no recipes for curry - the authors didn't seem overly fond of the cuisine and specifically stated in their volume:

"The following native dishes have been added by request. It may be mentioned incidentally that most native recipes are inordinately greasy and sweet, and that your native cooks invariably know how to make them well."

It would appear however, that the general resolve of most was to eat like the locals, and this may in fact have ensured their good health in such a hot foreign climate. Scientists have since proven that the spices common in curries such as cumin, allspice, cardamom, ginger, garlic and capsicum all have natural anti-bacterial properties, which would have

preserved meat and kept contaminating germs away for longer than more traditional British fare. We also now think that there are huge health benefits of eating lots of turmeric, which is a common ingredient in curries, as its active compound, Curcumin can help prevent both cancer and Alzheimer's. So perhaps this proves how humans can instinctively know which foods are good for them and may also explain why so many of us crave a curry?

It didn't take long for British tastes to become accustomed to Indian cuisine and it seems that those returning to Britain and its plainer bills of fare, keenly felt the withdrawal of spicy food. Recipe books in the 19th century start including more curry and Indian inspired recipes, many of which were contributed by those who had actually lived in India and could vouch for their authenticity. Mary Jewry in her book Warnes Model Cookery of 1871 proudly states:

"The author has the pleasure of offering in the next few pages original receipts, direct from the East, presented to her by Anglo-Indian friends. Some of the dishes are quite unknown in England."

Before long, the craze for curry swept the middle class homes of England, helped not only by returning ex-pats but even Queen Victoria herself – who as Empress of India, embraced the people, architecture and the culinary arts of perhaps her favourite colony. In her later years she befriended and some would say mothered a native Indian called Mohammed Abdul Karim, who came to England as a gift to serve as a waiter. He soon became a friend to the aging Queen, who had great respect for him, affectionately naming him "the Munshi" meaning teacher as he taught her Urdu and Hindi. She also had Indian staff to cook Indian cuisine everyday and wrote in her diary how they had served her a good curry.

Amazingly the first Indian restaurant called The Hindostanee Coffee House was opened in London in 1810, it even served takeaway meals, but it closed a few years later as although the food was popular, people generally preferred to eat food cooked at home by their own staff. Often Ex-pats imported their favourite spices or ready-made curry powder from contacts in India and instructed their cooks on how to make their favourite dishes. Generally though the reputation for British curries during the 19th century was dire. Mr Eliot-James, the author of a piece in Cassells Household Guide of 1912 entitled "Something about Curries" describes how difficult it was to find a good curry in Britain.

"A Badly made curry is an abomination, but oh! How rarely one has the good fortune to meet with one that is really well compounded."

He goes on to tell the tale of one particular rare dish of fine curry which he had eaten at the home of a retired Anglo-Indian General.

"I ventured to ask how my host could get his cook to make in England a curry so resembling those made in India, as I felt certain I detected some of the ingredients therein which are most difficult to procure here. He said laconically, "Parcel-post", adding, as a rider, that he had taught his cook how to make curry, and putting it with somewhat of a wail in his voice: "She's going to be married next month." I grasped the situation at once."

It even appears that during the 19th century some British people became almost addicted to the extreme spiciness of some Indian food and began to up the heat of traditional dishes to ferocious levels unknown in India, a practice this quote from *Philosophy in The Kitchen, 1885* proves. It warns against the overuse of capsicum:

"Over indulgence in condiments should be carefully avoided, as it is certainly injurious to health. Doctor Edward Smith, in his classical book on foods truly observes that: *The use of currie is less necessary and defeasible in a temperate than in a hot climate, and it is rare for one in England to tolerate the quantity of capsicum which is relished in India.* I have been occasionally invited in England to partake of curries hotter than the hottest Indian, yet which my Amphitryons would not scruple to call mild as mother's milk."

(Amphitryon, was a Theban general in ancient Greece who accidently killed his Father-in-law, so the quote suggests that his hosts served curries so hot they had the capability of killing!)

I haven't found any Victorian curry recipes, which could be this hot, and even the most authentic looking, rarely contained significant amounts of heat inducing ingredients. It has been proved however, that chillies are mildly addictive and I am sure that the challenge of making hotter and hotter curries, as their taste buds acclimatised to the endorphin inducing burn would have been as impossible to resist for the Victorians (particularly single gents?) as it is today!

VICTORIAN CURRY RECIPES

Most Victorian curry recipes were simple sauces made from ready made curry powder and stock and they were particularly seen as a good way of using up leftover meat from the Sunday Roast. Mutton curry was popular as was chicken, veal, fish, oxtail and rabbit and there are also a surprising amount of recipes for vegetarian curries, which were popular side dishes. Most of the recipes would only have tasted as good as the curry powder used to make them and so, it is hard to tell how palatable they were. For those who couldn't get their curry powder posted to them from India they could buy it from the many British grocers and chemists, who already sold spices for medicinal purposes and who started selling their own concoctions, although true curry aficionados would have thought them bland.

There were also, many 19th century curry recipes, which didn't rely on ready made curry powder and used instead, complex combinations of spices that were prepared and cooked from scratch. These were often very close to what would have been served in India and often included the addition of coconut milk and grated coconut in the sauce. Sometimes the recipes include strange ingredients such as sour apples and even rhubarb, which must have been English, sourced taste replacements for authentic Indian ingredients, which maybe needed to be used fresh, and so were not easily available in England before airfreight.

MY HOME MADE VICTORIAN CURRY BANQUET

I have a large collection of Victorian cookery books and after years of reading the many curry recipes they held and assuming that they wouldn't taste very nice, I decided to try them out for myself. So after perusing over 50 cookery books written between 1830 and 1923 I finally choose 5 recipes, which I would cook, for my family when I invited them to a Victorian curry banquet...

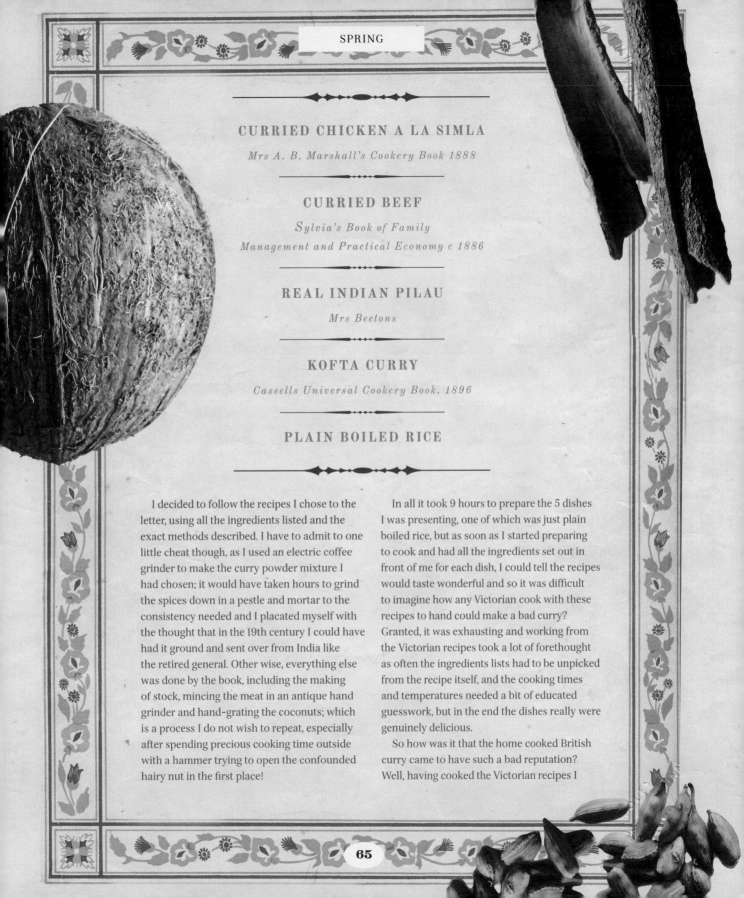

CURRIED CHICKEN A LA SIMLA

Mrs A. B. Marshall's Cookery Book 1888

CURRIED BEEF

*Sylvia's Book of Family
Management and Practical Economy c 1886*

REAL INDIAN PILAU

Mrs Beetons

KOFTA CURRY

Cassells Universal Cookery Book, 1896

PLAIN BOILED RICE

I decided to follow the recipes I chose to the letter, using all the ingredients listed and the exact methods described. I have to admit to one little cheat though, as I used an electric coffee grinder to make the curry powder mixture I had chosen; it would have taken hours to grind the spices down in a pestle and mortar to the consistency needed and I placated myself with the thought that in the 19th century I could have had it ground and sent over from India like the retired general. Other wise, everything else was done by the book, including the making of stock, mincing the meat in an antique hand grinder and hand-grating the coconuts; which is a process I do not wish to repeat, especially after spending precious cooking time outside with a hammer trying to open the confounded hairy nut in the first place!

In all it took 9 hours to prepare the 5 dishes I was presenting, one of which was just plain boiled rice, but as soon as I started preparing to cook and had all the ingredients set out in front of me for each dish, I could tell the recipes would taste wonderful and so it was difficult to imagine how any Victorian cook with these recipes to hand could make a bad curry? Granted, it was exhausting and working from the Victorian recipes took a lot of forethought as often the ingredients lists had to be unpicked from the recipe itself, and the cooking times and temperatures needed a bit of educated guesswork, but in the end the dishes really were genuinely delicious.

So how was it that the home cooked British curry came to have such a bad reputation? Well, having cooked the Victorian recipes I now have a few theories; I think the range of spices needed to make the best curries would have been too expensive or unavailable to most families and even if they could access them, they most probably wouldn't have been very fresh. I think that to many a housewife and cook the ingredients list would have also seemed a sheer extravagance and their instinct would have been to pare down the list of ingredients and replace key ingredients with others which were more economical or for items they already had to hand. I feel sure that most Victorian cooks would have been unable to imagine the importance of each individual spice in building up the depth and complexity of flavour required for a good curry and so instead of following the recipes precisely as I did, would have done what the British do best – they used their common sense and made do with what they had, while at the same time perhaps tweaking the final dish so that it wasn't too spicy, too hot or even too Indian.

I also doubt that many Victorian household cooks had any genuine interest in being able to cook a good curry and were unwilling to spend the time required in its authentic preparation. Their suspicions regarding this strange foreign food, which was so different from anything they knew would have clouded their judgement and they probably had no desire to eat it themselves. I am sure many would have been happy to serve any dish as a curry if it included at least some curry powder and as long as it didn't taste too much like their usual meat stew. Such dishes would pass muster with the family they worked for, after all, most people didn't know what a good curry should actually taste like anyway and believing that their cook had followed the recipe they had given them, would accept the dish and grow accustomed to how it tasted, that is until they got to taste a genuinely good curry for themselves.

The only way to know how to make a good curry is to first taste one, which anyone who had lived in India would have and so unless they maintained strict control of the ingredients and the method of cooking, the British curry would always disappoint. So my theory is that there were two types of curry eaters in the 19th and early 20th centuries – those who knew and loved the real thing and those who thought they knew what a good curry was. Those who knew a good curry were often too polite to tell those who didn't that they had got it wrong as this quote from Anglo-Indian, Mr Eliot-James in 1912 confirms:

"One is called on to eat and pass opinion on the most inferior concoctions because "you've been in India, dear and you must know how a curry ought to taste," and your hostess after a pause, during which you are mentally consigning that said curry to – oblivion, or anywhere so that you may never be asked to partake of it again, presses the question as to how you like it, adding some remark as, "I am always praised for my curries" so handicapped, you are obliged to tell a polite society story, unless you are one of those people who think it praiseworthy to blurt out objectionable truths without regard to other people's feelings."

As the 20th century progressed, those with real experience of a good curry started to dwindle as the Indian Empire crumbled, or perhaps they are happier to keep the secret to themselves? Either way, it is not until Indian immigrants to Britain start opening up their famous curry houses in the 1950s that all Brits had the opportunity to experience a more authentic taste of India and start to enjoy it as much as the old colonials had before them.

So my conclusion is that a good British

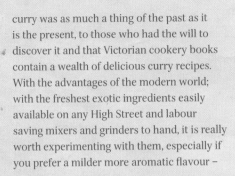

curry was as much a thing of the past as it is the present, to those who had the will to discover it and that Victorian cookery books contain a wealth of delicious curry recipes. With the advantages of the modern world; with the freshest exotic ingredients easily available on any High Street and labour saving mixers and grinders to hand, it is really worth experimenting with them, especially if you prefer a milder more aromatic flavour –

although there is nothing to prevent a chilli fiend from turning up the heat to give them the extra kick they crave.

I have included the recipes for the curries I cooked below, along with some modern advice. I have also added a few more recipes which I thought looked interesting, but I haven't managed to sample yet; If you feel inspired to give any of them a try, do get in touch and let me know how you got on.

CURRY POWDER AND SAUCES

CURRIE POWDER
Philosophy in the Kitchen 1885

I chose this recipe as it had an interesting mix of ingredients, and used an electric coffee grinder to make the powder fine. It is by far the best curry powder I have ever smelt. Although it isn't very hot, it gave a lovely deep multi-layered flavour to the dishes I used it in. I will be making it again, but may use fewer cloves in the next batch!

The Original Recipe

Take three-quarter of an ounce of ground black pepper, pimento (allspice) and cloves, and grated nutmeg, half and ounce of cayenne – which is amply sufficient – and twelve ounces of turmeric, and mix these ingredients well together. Now for the essential feature of the process, which consists of this – instead of using the ordinary mill ground powders of the seeds of cumin, coriander, caraway, cardamom and fenugreek, take two ounces and a half each of cumin and coriander seeds, one and a half ounces each of caraway and cardamom seeds and half ounce of fenugreek and roast them together in a clean frying pan over a slow fire, with diligent stirring. Grind the hot seeds, and mix the hot powder thoroughly with the turmeric mixture. This modification of the process serves to give the

currie a much more mellow flavour, When the currie powder has cooled, put it into well-corked small glass bottles.

Modern adaption for smaller amount

Mix together the following:
¾ teaspoon ground black pepper, allspice, ground cloves and grated nutmeg, ½ teaspoon cayenne pepper, 12 teaspoons turmeric.

Roast 2 teaspoons cumin and coriander seeds, 1 ½ teaspoons caraway, cardamom and fenugreek seeds, in a frying pan until they release their aroma, then grind into a powder.

Combine all the above and store in a glass screw lid jar.

CURRIED CHICKEN A LA SIMLA

This chicken curry recipe is taken from Mrs A.B. Marshall's Cookery Book of 1888. Mrs Agnes Marshall was an amazing Victorian cookery entrepreneur, who not only wrote cookery books, but sold her own branded ingredients, such as curry powder, her own brand of kitchen equipment and also ran a cookery school. I chose this recipe as I like the variety of ingredients and the fact it contained tamarinds and I was keen to see what they tasted like. The dish was rather laborious to make, but with a few modern short cuts wouldn't be a problem at all and it was really nice, the sauce had a slightly soured creamy taste, which I really enjoyed. I have included the original recipe as I didn't find it too hard to follow, just make a list of the ingredients before you start.

The Original Recipe

Pick, singe, and cleanse a chicken and cut it up in neat joints. Put into a stew pan two ounces of butter or dripping, with four onions that are cut up small, two sour apples, two bay leaves and a sprig of thyme chopped fine. Put the chicken into the pan, and season it with a saltspoonful of ground ginger, the same of mignonette pepper (equal amount of black and white peppercorns) and salt, one or two crushed Jamaica peppercorns (allspice) a dessertspoonful of tamarinds, a saltspoonful of coriander powder, a teaspoonful of turmeric powder; the same of chutney, and a saltspoonful of coralline (Cayenne) pepper. Fry for about fifteen minutes, and then add one ounce of crème de riz (rice flour), half a grated coconut, and the milk of a whole one, and the juice of one large or two small lemons. Cover the ingredients with one quart of water or stock, and boil gently for half and hour. Mix in a basin and ounce of crème de riz (rice flour) with a quarter of a pint of water or stock and stir it into the mixture till it boils, draw the pan to the side of the stove and let it simmer for about ten minutes, then remove the joints of chicken from the pan and keep them warm. Have the sauce well rubbed through a hair sieve or tammy, then re-boil it up; dish up the joints of chicken on a hot dish in a pile and pour the sauce all over it, garnish around the dish alternately with bunches of grated coconut (that has been warmed between two plates) and bunches of the compote of sultanas and have boiled rice on a plate. This dish can also be served foe an entrée or in place of roast game or poultry.

CURRIED BEEF
Sylvia's Book of Family Management
and Practical Economy, c1886

I chose to cook this recipe as it was so simple, of course its success depended on the quality of the curry powder, but the Victorian curry powder I had chosen to make really worked with this, I have since made it with leftover cold meat as the recipe suggests and with raw stewing steak and the latter turned out much nicer, with the meat taking on all of the curry flavour.

Ingredients

A few slices tolerably lean cold roast or boiled beef. 3 oz dripping, 2 onions, 1 wineglassful of beer, 1 dessertspoonful curry-powder.

Cut the beef into pieces about 1 inch square; put the dripping into a stewpan with the onions sliced and fry them a light brown colour. Add the other ingredients, and stir gently over a brisk fire for about 10 minutes, more beer or a spoonful or two of gravy or water, may be added; but a good curry should not be very thin. Place it in a deep dish with an edging of dry boiled rice.

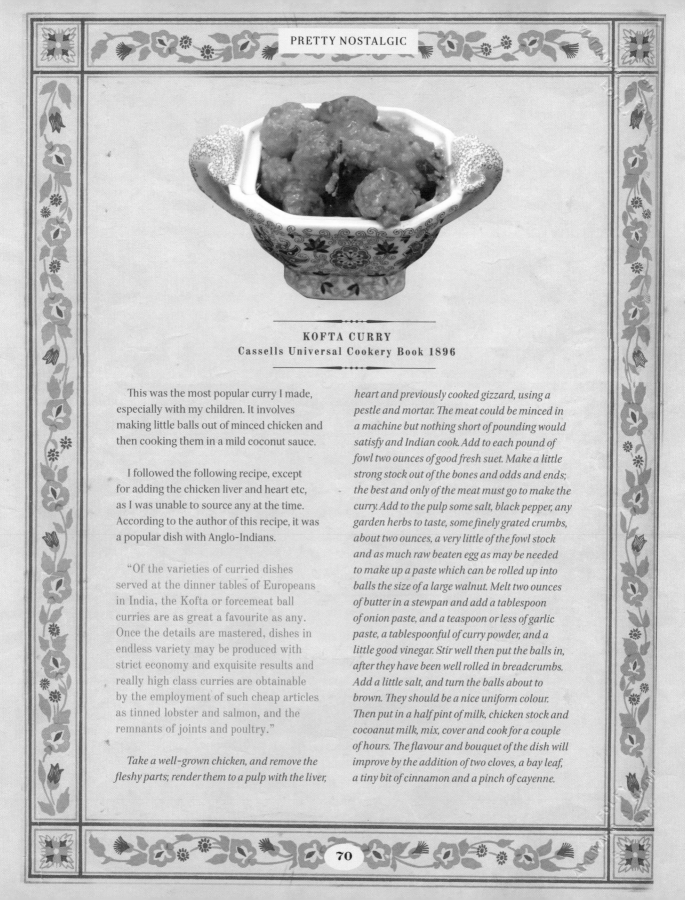

KOFTA CURRY
Cassells Universal Cookery Book 1896

This was the most popular curry I made, especially with my children. It involves making little balls out of minced chicken and then cooking them in a mild coconut sauce.

I followed the following recipe, except for adding the chicken liver and heart etc, as I was unable to source any at the time. According to the author of this recipe, it was a popular dish with Anglo-Indians.

"Of the varieties of curried dishes served at the dinner tables of Europeans in India, the Kofta or forcemeat ball curries are as great a favourite as any. Once the details are mastered, dishes in endless variety may be produced with strict economy and exquisite results and really high class curries are obtainable by the employment of such cheap articles as tinned lobster and salmon, and the remnants of joints and poultry."

Take a well-grown chicken, and remove the fleshy parts; render them to a pulp with the liver, heart and previously cooked gizzard, using a pestle and mortar. The meat could be minced in a machine but nothing short of pounding would satisfy and Indian cook. Add to each pound of fowl two ounces of good fresh suet. Make a little strong stock out of the bones and odds and ends; the best and only of the meat must go to make the curry. Add to the pulp some salt, black pepper, any garden herbs to taste, some finely grated crumbs, about two ounces, a very little of the fowl stock and as much raw beaten egg as may be needed to make up a paste which can be rolled up into balls the size of a large walnut. Melt two ounces of butter in a stewpan and add a tablespoon of onion paste, and a teaspoon or less of garlic paste, a tablespoonful of curry powder, and a little good vinegar. Stir well then put the balls in, after they have been well rolled in breadcrumbs. Add a little salt, and turn the balls about to brown. They should be a nice uniform colour. Then put in a half pint of milk, chicken stock and cocoanut milk, mix, cover and cook for a couple of hours. The flavour and bouquet of the dish will improve by the addition of two cloves, a bay leaf, a tiny bit of cinnamon and a pinch of cayenne.

REAL INDIAN PILAU
Beetons Book of Household Management 1923

This dish is a complete Indian meal in itself and it looked wonderful dished up on a large meat plate and decorated with boiled eggs, almonds and baby onions. The rice cooked with the minced onions was very tasty and I would certainly cook rice this way again.

Ingredients

Three onions, four or five cloves; a very small piece of cinnamon; a quarter of a pound of butter, three quarters of a pound of rice; one fowl or meat; six or seven hard-boiled eggs; tow ounces of almonds; two ounces of raisins, small onions.

Take the onions, cloves and a small piece of cinnamon, and with the butter fry them together then put in the rice and let it fry with them, but not to make it brown. Boil a fowl or a piece of meat, and with the gravy instead of water put it with the rice to boil, taking care to always have two inches of the gravy above the rice. When the rice is half done, put the fowl or meat into the middle of it, and let it remain over a gentle fire till sufficiently done and dry; then take it up, put it into a deep dish, cover the fowl all over with the rice and garnish it with the hard-boiled eggs cut in quarters, the almonds blanched, and the raisins, cloves and a few small boiled onions.

IT'S A COLOURFUL *life*

We sent Nostalgianeer *Corinne Young* on an assignment to interview the world famous textile designer Kaffe Fasset

72

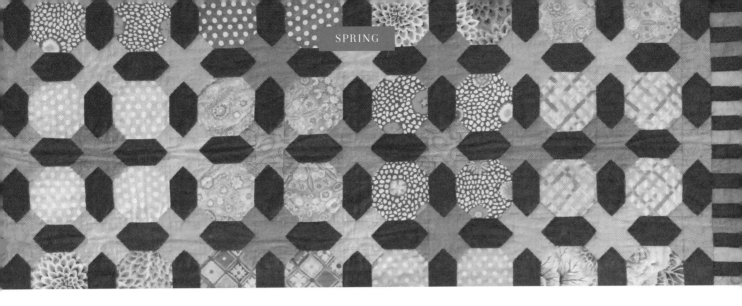

I have been a huge fan of Kaffe Fassett's work since my mother bought me his Glorious Knitting book 30 years ago. Since then I have acquired several more books, kits & fabrics, watched his television series on Channel 4, and been to several exhibitions, the latest of which was the wonderful 'A Life in Colour' at the Fashion and Textile Museum in 2013. Kaffe's work showed me the possibilities in working with textiles and ignited a passion, which resulted in my eventual study for a textile degree and then becoming a textile artist.

Imagine my delight then when The Nostalgianeers contacted me to ask me if I wanted to meet and interview Kaffe, as part of his 'Ancestral Gifts' exhibition at the, now closed, Quilt Museum in York - I could hardly contain my excitement! Kaffe turned out to be every bit as interesting and fascinating as I had known he would be. Read on to discover more about the man himself.

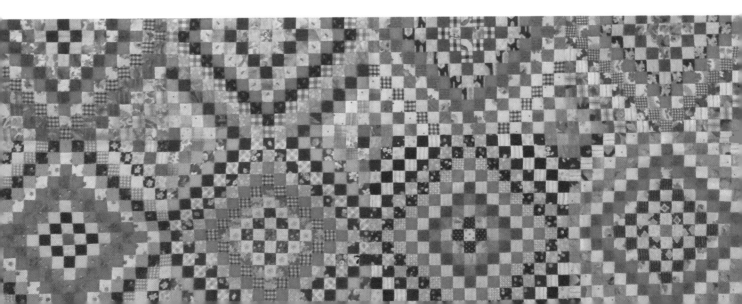

YOU WERE BORN AND GREW UP IN CALIFORNIA, WHAT FIRST ATTRACTED YOU TO VISIT ENGLAND?

The most obvious point is that I met Christopher Isherwood (The English Novelist), and he was just wonderful. I thought he was absolutely ancient and about to die, but he was about 17 years younger than I am now! He was so charismatic and full of life and he had a funny way of looking at the world. I bought all the books of his that I could get hold of, and I had a strong feeling that I wanted to go to that place that he was writing about. I also met lots of other English people, and I realised that they had a great sense of humour. So off I went for a couple of months vacation, and ended up staying for what is now over 50 years.

WHAT IS IT ABOUT ENGLAND THAT MADE YOU WANT TO MAKE YOUR PERMANENT HOME HERE?

I love the old worldiness of the place. Look at York where we are today! The old lanes, steeped in history and all the ancient architecture. This exhibition is of course looking at wonderful old British quilts. So all that and the fact that it is so close to Europe, (particularly Scandinavia) and Morocco. I jumped on a plane and went to Norway last week and before that we went to Prague, all that accessibility is wonderful – Paris is a favourite of course. Also there is something about the timing here. I have always been the impatient American, and I have learnt to be more tolerant, and listen a little more than I used to, and I find that I like to develop things slowly. The whole thing of being able to find textiles and develop them quietly without anyone making a song and dance about it. A

slower pace of life. The English are a little bit reticent and slower to come forward, but eventually you get a great reaction. Brandon was saying that I get a little impatient with my audience when they are quiet and don't respond, but they are just taking it in, and you get a really satisfactory feedback at the end. I have been able to develop my whole textile persona in a way that I wouldn't have been able to do in America. I think I would have become Walt Disney or some incredibly commercial person. It would all have been about manufacturing sheet collections, and the craft and the creative flow would have been lost. I am thrilled that being here has enabled me to put all this creativity into books too.

HOW IMPORTANT WAS IT FOR YOU TO FOLLOW A CREATIVE PATH. WAS THIS FROM CHILDHOOD? ALSO, YOU TRAINED AS A PAINTER, WHAT ATTRACTED YOU TO WORKING IN TEXTILES AND MADE YOU CHOSE IT AS YOUR MAIN WORKING MEDIUM?

I could have been a dancer, photographer, actor or any number of things; or of course a painter. My paintings have always been quite theatrical, lots of still lives, which are actually features on a stage.

However, I soon found knitting, and found that there wasn't anybody else doing anything with it! I had seen people doing some interesting things with knitting in America. There were a couple of guys there – we were all very poor – and they were going to the charity shops and buying old sweaters and unravelling them and making these wonderful striped sweaters – what you call 'dump' sweaters, and so that planted a seed in my head. I then found these fabulous yarns in Scotland, and

realised that everyone was going around in the most boring plain beige or black sweaters, and I thought what is wrong with everyone? Everyone could be using these yarns dyed with the most beautiful, vegetable dyed palettes. Wool takes colours so beautifully, and to take a pink yarn and mix it with rust and a bit of blue, and the combinations that you got with these wonderful Shetland yarns. At first I thought oh this is a big distraction, this is wasting time, and I must get back to painting. Then I gradually realised that I would rather work with textiles than anything else. Every step of the way was motivating then, and still is now. Even now I love sitting down with a new piece of knitting and following it through and living dangerously. I have taught my partner Brandon Mably to knit and now he is terrific.

DO YOU HAVE A FAVOURITE PERIOD IN HISTORY?

I do love architecture, and the more ancient it is the better I like it. I was recently working on costumes and sets for the Shakespeare play 'As you Like It' and looking into the Elizabethan period was fascinating. It must have been so flamingly creative with people making mad embroidered tops and stumpwork and it was really 'out there'.

DO YOU HAVE ANY FAVOURITE CURRENT ARTISTS, TEXTILE OR OTHERWISE?

I was always interested in anyone who was interested in colour. We were just in Austria and the Hundertwasser ethic is everywhere. That guy had such an influence on his generation of people. He is a big inspiration, and strangely enough Morandi, the Italian painter. His work is about as neutral as you can get. There is a touch of lavender, a little bit of pink or something and basically many shades of beige and I love them they are so restful. A lot of my work is quite subtle, though people don't believe it. Most people think everything I do is like Disney on acid, but I do really love a pale palette with gentle shifts of colour. I always start off my talks with lots of pale pieces.

WHEN YOU ARE IN YOUR STUDIO, WHAT IS A TYPICAL DAY, AND WHAT IS YOUR FAVOURITE ASPECT OF YOUR WORKING LIFE?

Being in my studio is my oxygen. I get up early about 6.30, go up to my studio and just get stuck in, and then have breakfast about 8 o clock. Then we decide what is happening during the day and where I have to be. I love it if I can stay in the studio all day. That is a real luxury. People say 'how do you get done what you get done' and I say well we hit the ground running. When we have time in the studio we use it, and really focus and get stuff done. There are other things that are exciting like when you have done 20 or 25 quilts, and you take them off to a location and you start seeing them against a wonderful old building, and place them where they are going to look fabulous and that's exciting. And then it's wonderful making a book about it, putting that together. Exhibitions are such a joy because our stuff is folded up in cupboards most of the time. Its great to get them down, shake them out, hang them and light them. These are the best moments, and then when everybody comes, that is a whole other thing. Then you have to deal with people's reactions to the work. But I love just

seeing the quilts in the peace of this place (the Quilt Museum), and how they relate to each other and to the old pieces in some way.

DO YOU HAVE A FAVOURITE PIECE OF YOUR WORK, AND WHAT DO YOU WANT PEOPLE TO FEEL WHEN THEY LOOK AT YOUR WORK?

Not really, I always think of what Picasso said when he was asked the same question and he said 'what I am working on now'. You always want what you do to be the best. I think I am constantly moving on. Sometimes I get a great shock when I see a painting that I did years ago. You know when I come across it, I wonder how I was able to achieve that, but I am always just trying to move on.

It is incredibly difficult to choreograph how people view your work, and whatever expectations you have, people usually go in a different direction. What I want is for people to get the same buzz out of my work that I get out of an old quilt. I hope that they get an idea for a fabulous border on a sweater, or a way to do something in their room or to make a quilt, but to do it in their own way. Some people slavishly go out and find exactly what fabrics I've used, or which yarns I've used and they are so proud of what they have made and show it to you, and my immediate thought is what am I supposed to be reacting to? Of course they are showing you their skill, and they are so proud of what they made - to them its spectacular, and then I'm there – I understand. More often people give it their own twist and choose their own fabrics, or do a completely new colour scheme. When I give my workshops we take one quilt and 30

people do an entirely different interpretation of that quilt. When it's a really good workshop, people get really into it and kick off their shoes and go to work! In the talk tonight I will be showing examples of the kinds of things that I love and treasure. I want people to look at an old quilt the way I look at them, and take enough out of it that they can make something of their own, and really flex their creative muscles.

REGARDING THE CURRENT IMPORTANCE OF REUSING AND RECYCLING, HOW DO YOU RECYCLE IN YOUR STUDIO? FOR INSTANCE, IF YOU ARE NO LONGER HAPPY WITH A SWEATER DO YOU TAKE IT APART AND REKNIT IT?

Not so much with the knitting. I have given a lot of my little sample bits of fabric to appliquers who have made a rough appliqué out of it. I am just working on a quilt at the moment which is very bold stripes put together and some of that is old furnishing fabrics and old workmen's shirts that I have been collecting, and then someone gave me a collection of old shirts that they had bought in charity shops and so all that's going into a quilt

CAN YOU TELL ME A LITTLE ABOUT YOUR WORK FOR THIS EXHIBITION?

At first the exhibition was going to be based on my wonderful collection of old quilts because I was dying to show them to everyone and I thought – great here is a chance - but then we started thinking about it and one of the curators here said "do you think you could think about making a couple of quilts that are inspired by our collection?" I then went to look at the collection

and I thought OMG! My mind just burst and I realised I could make a whole book based on this collection, and the whole thing just fell into place. The collection is just so fruity and scrappy and all the things that I love. It is wild extraneous worlds coming together, and lots of it. There's nothing restrained or grown up, its just gypsy. My heart is in these quilts that have memories. You know that a life has been led while making them. The little crib quilt is a little brown mousey thing, its sort of stained and old and faded but when you look at it it's all these tiny little pieces of squared fabric sown together so carefully. To me it says somebody had a lot of ill friends and spent hours by their beds with a little purse containing these tiny pieces of fabric and needles and threads. Because what is better than being quietly there for someone. In the past I visited several of my friends in hospital with Aids, I would sit quietly in the hospital just knitting and we both felt so soothed and the much better for it.

WHAT IS YOUR VIEW ON THE IMPORTANCE OF TRADITIONAL SKILLS? AS I AM SURE YOU KNOW IN THIS COUNTRY WE ARE IN DANGER OF LOSING OUR TRADITIONAL SKILLS, WHAT DO YOU THINK CAN BE DONE ABOUT THIS?

My feeling is that you (the UK) will get over it, and get back to it. A while ago Americans were obsessed with their hair and shoes, their place in society and celebrities or technology , and all that was very strange to me. But now we are over it, and we are again in love with the hands and what they can do and all the homemade crafts, and finding beautiful fabrics and putting them together. It is so alive, and the tools of quilting are so beautiful. Now you can get tools that cut several layers of fabric at a time accurately, and guides for millimetre perfect sewing, and you learn all the time. I say to people at my workshops that you have stumbled across one of the greatest crafts there is. Quilting is just evolving all the time. It's so alive and everybody wants to help everybody else. It's not one of those things that one person has the secret and no one shows anybody.

WHAT IS THE BEST PIECE OF ADVICE YOU CAN GIVE TO SOMEONE WHO WANTS TO FOLLOW A CREATIVE PATH LIKE AN ARTIST OR DESIGNER JUST STARTING OUT.

I would say don't be afraid of colour because a lot of people are so timid about it. I would say plunge in, be vulgar, go over the top and enjoy yourself. Pretend you are a child who has discovered a wonderful muddy puddle and get in and get dirty. I hate it when people are so cautious. On the other hand I love restraint and doing things that are very 'whispery', but there is a lot of colour and variety in there. I love just looking at the stone in the architecture in York and seeing all those wonderful colours. Don't be lazy, go out and find it. Even in neutral palettes you will find a lot of colour vibration in there with different levels of pattern. The tiny shifts in colour just make a piece come alive.

You can view Corinne's textile art on her website **corinneyoungtextiles.co.uk.**

SOAP
cleaned up

Crafting natural cleansing
bars from her garden
workshop, artisan soap maker
Seona Reilly shares why she
became smitten with soap

I'M LUCKY TO LIVE A LOVELY LIFE IN A RURAL CHESHIRE VILLAGE WITH MY FAMILY, A COUPLE OF CHICKENS AND HECTOR THE DOG. MY DAYS ARE BUSY IN MY GARDEN WORKSHOP, CREATING NATURAL, SOOTHING AND ENHANCING SKINCARE PRODUCTS. FROM INGREDIENTS WE ALL CAN READ AND UNDERSTAND - INSPIRED BY MY NATURAL ENVIRONMENT.

WOULD YOU EAT IT?

My soap story began some time ago. I have always been interested in natural products as it's believed that our bodies absorb up to 60% of the products we put on our skin. For me, being as careful about what we put on our bodies is as important as what we eat and put inside them. And having children really focused my attention on the subject.

TIME FOR A CHANGE

From being a tiny baby, our son suffered with severe eczema and, as advised by medics, we diligently but warily applied topical steroids and emollients, which appeared to calm his sore skin but never really seemed to solve the underlying problem. One day, whilst looking to understand his condition further, I stumbled across an article suggesting that whilst the topical steroid in the cream temporarily calmed his inflamed skin, some creams and emollients could in fact be exacerbating his condition. The article revealed that many creams used for the relief of skin conditions contain petroleum, synthetic dyes, fragrances and chemical preservatives. I also discovered that the water in many creams -included as a bulking agent and to aid absorption - was in fact drying my son's skin further as it evaporated from the very lotion we were using to soothe his skin.

With clean living firmly on the agenda, these days people regularly read labels to check ingredients in their food, scanning for hidden sugars and edible nasties.

However I believe that when it comes to skincare, consumers are much less aware. Blinded by the science most consumers rarely look beyond the packaging and claims for skin rejuvenation, unaware they could be absorbing unwanted chemicals into their bodies.

NATURE KNOWS BEST

After researching more natural alternatives I began experimenting with ingredients I had in my kitchen cupboard - making a gentle, preservative-free moisturising cream from simple natural ingredients I had in my pantry. A super-gentle, water-free balm containing nourishing Coconut oil - then an underused ingredient but now a superfood, hugely trendy (and more expensive!) thanks to health food icons and bloggers extolling its virtues. I was delighted to find that my home-spun cream really worked and my son's skin was calmed and soothed.

For ease of transport, I then created an equally moisturising lotion bar from similar oils, which is solid at room temperature but leaves a lovely moisturising layer when warmed in the hands and gently rubbed over the skin (the recipe for which is in the adjacent box.) It's really useful, can be cut into travel size pieces, and is something my family wouldn't now be without.

Following my success with creams and lotion bars, I got braver and started experimenting with natural, cold process soap making. After a couple of failed batches I got the hang of it and fell head over heels in love with

natural, chemical free soap and the magical alchemy of soap making. Using super-moisturising oils such as starflower and apricot kernel I created a soap that miraculously didn't exacerbate - and in fact calmed - my child's skin.

SCIENCE MEETS SKIN

Now being completely hooked on cold process soap making, I continued to experiment, creating different recipes for different soaps, varying the base oils and pure essential oils to create a vast array of different textured and scented soaps, which I gave away to friends and family for Christmas (and any other reason I could find!)

Over time I played with and perfected my soap recipes, avidly researching the therapeutic properties of essential oils and the characteristics of different natural oils and butters - how they impact the firmness, lather and conditioning qualities of soap. Simultaneously, the early recipients of my soaps, creams and lotion bars began placing orders for more, so I was inspired to not only accommodated those requests but to tentatively venture to a local artisan market with my soaps where they were enthusiastically received - and from that response my then business, English Garden Soaps, was born. Early on it was difficult to gauge supply and demand, particularly as curing times can vary due to humidity levels, and some time I ran out of customers' favourites. I remember one particular lady who told me that she flatly refused to tell her friends where she

bought the 'miracle soap' she raved to them about, in case they were to buy the last available bar and I wouldn't have any ready for her. It was flattering but not great for business!

THEN CAME PARIS

In 2004, we went to live in a village west of Paris for a few years, where I found a loyal following of both French and ex-pat customers at local markets. This enabled me to fine tune my range according to which had the most kerb appeal on my stall. It was interesting to see what sold well and who bought what - women flocked to my gentle, scented, moisturising soaps, whilst men tended to go for my salt scrub bars, buying them in bulk!

WORKSHOP WONDER

Returning to England in 2008, I continued to make and sell my natural soaps at local markets. As demand increased my business outgrew our family kitchen (which had been taken over by teenage boys constantly rummaging for food!) and we built a lovely soap-making workshop in the garden - my dedicated shrine to all things scented and soapy! It's bliss - if I'm missing, then I'm probably hiding in there, concocting intoxicating fragrance blends and therapeutic products; experimenting with botanicals and other natural additions such as organic honey or clay. Work doesn't really get much better than this!

My soap making has become a wonderful labour of love, the patient weeks of waiting for the soaps to cure are the absolute antithesis of the quick fix, fast paced world we all live in. Although my business has expanded, I still make my soap in small, manageable batches, hand stirring the oils, mixing in natural, muted colourants and sprinkling each loaf of soap batter with botanicals such as flower petals or citrus peel to create a pretty or striking topping to the soap. Once cured the edges of each individual bar are hand beveled - which gives each one a genuinely unique look (quite different from the symmetrical commercial bars found in the supermarket!) - before being carefully wrapped and labelled. I'm always on the look out for inventive new toppings and experimenting with flowers and seeds from my garden - my workshop is filled with various herbs and flowers just 'hanging' out ready to be used.

DOWN TO BUSINESS

At outside markets I sometimes sell from 'Morris' - my beloved 1968 Morris traveller. He draws a crowd and customers often reminisce about their childhood memories in their parents' Morris Traveller (they usual recall how an uncomfortable amount of small children were squeezed in the back!) I usually only take Morris to markets in the summer months however, in the hope that the weather will be kind to us, because he doesn't like to get his wooden frame too wet (or rather, I don't like him to, because I'm the one who has to rub him dry later on!) Also, doing markets in the rain isn't great – soap and water is not a great mix until you get them to your bathroom!

The thrill I get from seeing my soaps head off to new homes is pretty fantastic, and hearing my customers tell me what a difference my soaps have made to their skin makes all the hard work worthwhile. Compliance with European legislation can be an arduous task. The regulations regarding the manufacture and sale of skincare products changed in 2013 and many small, independent soap makers weren't able to absorb the resulting costs, or find the time for the addition administrative tasks, and so closed down as a result, which is a real shame for the skilled artisan soap market.

Fortunately I was well enough established to survive, and recently, after a lot of requests and planning, I have decided to expand my product range to include my natural creams and balms alongside my soaps. I am therefore in the process of incorporating the English Garden Soaps range within my new, exciting venture, Village Alchemist - a skincare line reflective of the magical process of natural soap making and skincare, all still formulated and lovingly made in small batches in my beautiful village garden workshop.

Discover Village Alchemist online
villagealchemist.co.uk
Instagram: village_alchemist
Facebook: villagealchemistuk

START YOUR OWN SOAP STORY

Fancy having a go at making your own soap? I've included a simple recipe for you to try. Although you shouldn't alter the oil to lye ratio, you could add your own choice of essential oil for a lovely fragrant soap. Remember to check with the supplier however for any potential allergens that the essential oil contains if you are prone to skin sensitivity. Although natural, many oils contain allergens that some people are sensitive to. For example, geraniol, limonene and linalool are found in lavender essential oil, whilst rose absolute is also a source of citronellol, farnesol and eugenol.

You can also get creative with colour as soaps can be imbued with natural ingredients such as carrot powder for an orange hue, coffee or cocoa powder for a earthy brown shade, powdered ginger, paprika or curry powder for a pretty peach, madder root results in pale pink or spirulina for a gorgeous, muted green.

You could also add some ground pomace, dried citrus peel or oats for a more scrubby bar - they make perfect yet gentle exfoliators.

Have fun with them, be instinctive and I'm sure you'll be thrilled with your soap.

IN THE BOXES - THE ALCHEMY OF TRADITIONAL SOAP-MAKING (A BASIC CHEMISTRY LESSON!)

I make soap using the traditional age-old, cold-process method. It involves mixing a lye solution with moisturising vegetable oils and butters, such as coconut oil and shea butter. This causes a natural chemical reaction called saponification, whereby the sodium in the Sodium Hydroxide (an alkali) bonds with individual fatty acids in the oil (a mild acid) to create soap (the salt of the fatty acids), whilst simultaneously releasing glycerine - the humectant that makes handmade cold processed soap so naturally moisturising (the lovely glycerine is often extracted from commercially made soap, due to its high resale value.)

Once made, cold process soaps usually require between four to eight weeks to 'cure' on drying racks (I like to use apple racks), during which time the pH level continues to drop and the bars harden.

WHAT IS LYE? IS IT SAFE? WHY IS IT NOT ON THE INGREDIENTS LABEL?

Natural soap has been made with lye for over 5,000 years. All soap is made with the use of lye - it is used as an agent to create a chemical reaction - but the end product should never contain lye in its original form.

It is a caustic substance with the chemical name sodium hydroxide. Nowadays it is made in a lab by electrolysing water, which ensures purity and availability, but it was originally sourced from hardwood ashes.

Professional soap makers work from very precise formulations that carefully balance the ingredients to ensure that the soap is never 'lye heavy' (meaning that there was insufficient oil in the original mix to partner with the lye, leaving raw lye in the soap.) Most soap makers actually formulate recipes with a 'lye discount'

(also called superfatting) of around 5%, meaning that there will be 5% unsaponified oil in the finished product, to ensure there is no chance of any raw lye.

Because of the saponification process, lye does not exist in the finished product. And in fact, other than the unsaponified oils used for superfatting, the original base oils and butters don't exist in the soap in their original state either. This is because the lye is there purely to create a natural chemical reaction (attaching to the fatty acids in the base oils and splitting off the glycerine) whereby creating saponified oils - a kind of salt - which is then labelled as, for example, sodium olivate (from olive oil) and sodium Shea butterate (from, you guessed it, shea butter!)

Lye is extremely corrosive and needs to be handled with care. It's hygroscopic and needs to be kept in an airtight container, otherwise the moisture it absorbs can create an imbalance in recipes.

HOW DOES SOAP WORK?

Oils and fats contain mixtures of fatty acids, bonded together with the molecule glycerol (glycerine). The lye breaks the fatty acids away from the glycerol and converts the fatty acids into sodium salts, such as sodium olivate from olive oil. These salts act as 'surfactants' - substances that reduce the surface tension in liquids, forming tiny balls around particles of grease, stopping the grease from being hydrophobic and allowing it to dissolve and be carried away by water.

Super-moisturizing lotion bars to soothe problem skin

YOU WILL NEED:

- 1/4 cup Mango Butter or Shea Butter
- 1/3 cup Fermented Cod Liver Oil (fermented cod liver oil has fat soluble vitamins and Omega-3 fatty acids to help the skin heal and to nourish it)
- A few drops of essential oil (optional, and not advised on particularly sore skin)
- 1/4 cup Cocoa Butter
- 6 tablespoons of dry beeswax pellets

EQUIPMENT:

- A double boiler or a heat resistant bowl sitting in a small pan, not touching the bottom
- A plastic or wooden spoon for mixing
- Silicone cupcake/ muffin moulds or (preferably) plastic deodorant containers
- Paper towels or old rags that can be thrown away - it can get messy!

TO MAKE THE BARS:

1. Combine the butters and beeswax in the top of the double boiler or bowl.
2. Put about an inch of water in the bottom of the double boiler or pan and bring to the boil.
3. Reduce heat to a simmer and stir the mixture carefully until all ingredients have melted. Be careful not to get any water in the mixture.
4. Once all ingredients have melted, remove from heat and add essential oils and cod liver oil.
5. Stir, then carefully pour the mixture in to the moulds or deodorant tubes. Transfer them to the refrigerator to harden or let them sit on the counter top for a few hours hours to harden.

In warm weather it may be best to keep them in the fridge until required.

Make your own soap
N.B This recipe is superfatted at 5%

YOU WILL NEED:

- 300g Coconut oil
- 300g Palm oil
- 300g Olive oil
- 40g Castor oil
- 136g Lye
- 357g Distilled water

EQUIPMENT
(DON'T USE EQUIPMENT FOR SOAPMAKING THAT YOU HOPE TO STILL USE FOR FOOD PREPARATION)

- Heat-resistant glass, stainless steel, or Polypropylene plastic containers
- Rubber spatula
- 22cm -25cm long silicone loaf mould
- Accurate scales Stick blender
- Protective clothing - goggles, rubber gloves and mouth mask, along with long sleeved top, trousers and closed-toe shoes.

METHOD

1. Protect yourself from the lye with safety goggles, gloves and face mask. Ensure that you're wearing long sleeves and your feet are fully covered, and banish children and pets from the kitchen until after all the soap-making clearing up is done!

2. Measure out the lye and water in separate containers and then very carefully add the lye to the water, DO NOT add the water to the lye as it could erupt. Stir until the water turns clear and set aside somewhere safe. Do not breathe in the fumes. Be very careful not to splash any lye water on your skin. If you accidentally do so, rinse continuously with running water and seek medical assistance if necessary.

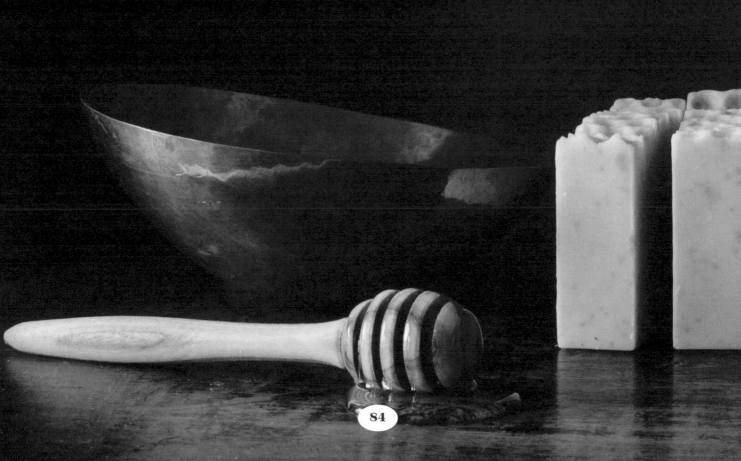

3. Measure out and melt the solid oils, then measure out the liquid oils and combine all.

4. Once the oils and the lye water have cooled to between 110 degrees F and 120 degrees F carefully pour the lye water into the oils.

5. Blend the soap batter with a stick blender until the soap reaches trace - a custard like consistency, recognisable by the trail left on the surface of the batter when the blender is taken out of the batter and drizzled across the top. If the trail remains for a second or two then you have trace, so don't blend anymore at this stage or the batter may seize and become unmanageable. If adding fragrance to your soap, hand stir it in well now.

6. Pour the soap batter into your mould. Cover the mould with cling film and leave to set for 24-48 hours. Then, wearing rubber gloves, unmould, cut into bars and leave to cure in a dry place for four to six weeks, turning the bars over regularly to help the drying process. Be patient here - the longer you wait before using the soap the firmer, less slimy and longer lasting the bar will be.

7. Before using your soap you may wish to zap test a bar to check whether the pH of the batch has dropped sufficiently to create mild and gentle soap. Simply place a bar of soap onto the tip of your tongue and if you feel a tingling sensation then the pH of your soap has not lowered sufficiently yet and should be left to cure for longer.

BOHEMIAN
rhapsody

A brief glimpse into the artistic and aesthetic world of the Bloomsbury group and their home, Charleston House.

WORDS: **KATJA DELL**
PHOTOGRAPHS: **PENELOPE FEWSTER AND TONY TREE**
COURTESY OF THE CHARLESTON TRUST

> *"Women have served all these centuries as looking-glasses possessing the magic and delicious power of reflecting the figure of man at twice its natural size."*
> **Virginia Woolf**

A PRIVILEGED CHILDHOOD

The Bloomsbury Group remains to this day the synonym for a pioneering way of thinking, and the private club where young avant-garde artists, writers and philosophers were given the freedom of expression so blatantly denied to them by the buttoned-up protocol of the day.

At the epicentre of this volcano of revolutionaries and free thinkers were two sisters, Vanessa Bell and Virginia Woolf.

Born in an upper-middle class Victorian family, to an esteemed writer as a father, and a mother with aristocratic roots, Vanessa's and Virginia's life was one of privilege.

When widowers Leslie Stephen and Julia Duckworth married, they already had four children between them. Vanessa, Virginia and their brothers Thoby and Adrian were the new offspring of the union.

A cramped house with eight growing children did not offer much scope for freedom and individuality, two essential rights that both sisters craved. The Stephens were an intellectual atheist family and believed in education for their daughters as well as their sons. Both sisters had access to the extensive family library and were taught mathematics, philosophy and science.

Nevertheless, it would prove hard to break the mould of the rigid patriarchal rules of the time, and a thirst for knowledge was considered unfeminine. The Stephen boys would be expected to carve out an eminent career for themselves, and the girls would be shown how to run a home.

Following the premature death of their mother and step sister Stella, the girls were left in the hands of a grieving and domineering father who could not always comprehend their needs, and the forward attentions of their incestuous half-brother George.

SENSE AND SENSIBILITY

"Broken asunder, yet made in the same mould, could it be that each completed what was dormant in the other?"
Virginia Woolf

Vanessa, the more pragmatic of the two sisters was the quiet and sensible mother figure. An introvert with a dreamy and melancholic expression, who often felt that she was dull and intellectually inadequate.
Her silent and secretive manners made her appear aloof, and hid her passionate, bohemian nature. In times of difficulty, she would seek solace in her painting or anything visually stimulating.

Virginia, the younger sister, was bright and articulate, but immature and in need of praise and attention. Fiercely jealous and possessive, she lived in constant fear of losing the affections of her beloved sister, frequently resorting to emotional blackmail to keep her close.

Virginia possessed an extraordinary wit and was a delightful conversationalist, consistently surrounded by a willing audience, but had suffered bouts of severe depression from an early age. She was terrified of mirrors and loathed her physical appearance. Despite their countless differences, they were bound by a profound degree of affection and solidarity.

NEW FOUND FREEDOM

"Lock up your libraries if you like; but there is no gate, no lock, no bolt that you can set upon the freedom of my mind."
Virginia Woolf

After their father's death, the Stephens decided to leave the gloominess of their Kensington family home and relocate to the less sophisticated district of Bloomsbury. At 46 Gordon Square, Vanessa was finally granted the freedom to unleash her artistic and creative potential by re-decorating her new home.

Thoby's Cambridge group of friends from Trinity College would often be invited to Vanessa's Friday Club soirees where they would discuss art, sex and politics without inhibition.

The newly formed Bloomsbury Group, largely inspired by the philosophy of G.E. Moore's "Principia Ethica", comprised the four Stephen siblings, art critic Clive Bell, biographer Lytton Strachey, political writer Leonard Woolf, economist Maynard Keynes, civil servant Saxon Sidney-Turner, editors Desmond and Molly MacCarthy, artist Duncan Grant and novelist E.M. Forster.

Any prudishness in terms of dress, conversation or opinion was quickly abandoned and the sisters were able to join in the debate. Several topics that would have been deemed preposterous or almost profane in more formal surroundings, were now liberally discussed.

Unlike most Bloomsbury members who were openly homosexual, Clive Bell's nonchalant flamboyance, his heterosexuality and elegant deportment made him an excellent candidate for Vanessa.

Vanessa liked Clive, but was reluctant to give up her independence. When her brother Thoby died, she finally capitulated and agreed to marry Bell. The initial marital bliss transformed her. She bloomed both sexually and artistically and her

confidence soared. In Virginia's eyes Vanessa had become a pagan fertility goddess. An ideal, that she would never achieve herself.

PROMISQUITY AND RIVALRY

> *"You have the children, the fame by rights belongs to me."*
> **Virginia Woolf**

Clive was quick to abandon the marital bed. His frequent escapades with other woman and the platonic love story with Virginia while acting as her literary critic and confidant enraged Vanessa, who was dedicating her time to the upbringing of her two sons Julian and Quentin.

The intellectual intimacy between her sister and husband, and Virginia's frequent remarks about writing being a superior art to painting was debilitating.

Vanessa vented her frustration by co-founding the Omega artistic movement with art critic and painter Roger Fry, with whom she embarked on a long affair. The Omega provided the platform for the post-impressionist artist movement and an opportunity for Vanessa to escape from her maternal duties and craft a serious artistic career for herself. Over time she became drawn to her friend and collaborator Duncan Grant. Duncan's attractive features, his vitality and unique vision for modern design greatly appealed to Vanessa.

Duncan however was homosexual. He had had a brief relationship with her brother Adrian and was in constant search for new lovers. While Vanessa craved stability, Duncan would only provide occasional sex and a flighty emotional attachment. The union produced a daughter, Angelica, who was deceived into believing her real father was Clive Bell.

During her early thirties even Virginia relinquished her spinsterhood and married activist Leonard Woolf. Virginia's fear of men, her changing moods and frigidity prevented her from embracing a fulfilling relationship. Her books were a surrogate for the children she would never have, and a means to experience at least part of the family utopia that her elder sister so unequivocally embodied.

In later years, Virginia's alleged lesbian tendencies made her seek the company of other female intellectuals. Her relationship with aristocrat and socialite Vita Sackville-West was masterfully related in her epic, Orlando.

COUNTRY LIVING

> *"I'm sure, if you get Charleston, you'll end up buying it for ever. If you live there, you could make it absolutely divine."*
> **Virginia Woolf**

During their childhood years, the only escape from the stifling oppressiveness of London, were the holidays at Talland House in St Ives.

The refreshing shabbiness of the interiors at Talland, the white washed houses and bright blues and yellows of the Cornish seaside were reflected in Virginia's novel "To the Lighthouse". Vanessa's more visual perception of their holiday house would inspire the interior design at her future East Sussex home – Charleston.

Leonard and Virginia acquired a printing press and were successfully running their publishing company, Hogarth Press, from their Sussex Country homes.

Virginia's persuasive powers combined with the need to have her sister close by meant that in 1916 Vanessa, Duncan and his lover Bunny took a lease from the Firle estate, and moved to Charleston.

According to Vanessa, Charleston was: "absolutely perfect, most lovely, very solid and simple with flat walls, a wonderful tiled roof and a beautiful pond with a willow at one side". She was in her element again and embraced the new decoration project with gusto.

Despite its beauty, the house was in a state

of disrepair and had no heating, electricity or running water. Through the joint efforts and creative talents of its new occupants the house soon became habitable and its blank canvas feel was enlivened by the cheerfulness of the Omega pottery, fabrics and furniture.

The opulent visual sensations and bohemian ambiance of this relatively humble country home appealed to its visitors. The circular table in the dining room hosted many an eminent artist and writer of the day. According to guests, the hospitality was excellent and informal, the food simple but appetising, and the drink flowed in abundance. The dark blue stencilled wallpaper was created free hand by Duncan, Quentin and Angelica and served as contrasting background for the Bloomsbury paintings and ceramics.

The Garden Room was where Lytton Strachey read extracts from his work "*Eminent Victorians*" causing Duncan Grant to fall asleep, and the room where Angelica was told that Duncan was her real father.

The Library was originally Vanessa's bedroom, but it

later became part of Clive Bell's living area. Its sombre appearance is brightened by Duncan's post-impressionist figures on the door panels and white bookcase.

The studio was the heart of the house, with its brightly coloured caryatids painted by Duncan, and Vanessa's tiles behind the stove. This large and welcoming gathering place was ideal for the former Bloomsbury set guests, where they would converse, listen to music and discuss new artistic trends. The large walnut cabinet still hosts a collection of Omega ceramics, and a bust of Virginia overlooks the room.

The Garden was the children's playing area, but also served as a source of food during the years of rationing.

THE WAR YEARS

> *"To see London all blasted, raked my heart."* **Virginia Woolf**

The period between the two World Wars brought desolation, destruction and loss.

Lytton Strachey died of cancer, shortly followed by his long-term companion and painter Dora Carrington who shot herself two months after his death. Vanessa's former lover and friend Roger Fry died unexpectedly after a fall at his London home. Only a few years later, Vanessa's eldest son Julian enrolled as a volunteer in the Spanish Civil War and was killed while driving an ambulance.

During the Blitz, the Bloomsbury district was badly hit and the sisters' London homes and possessions destroyed. Both Duncan Grant and Bunny Garnet were conscientious objectors and did not join the army, but helped with the war effort by farming the land.

Due to rationing, very little fuel was available, which made transport an occasional luxury. The need for basic provisions meant that the family had to economise and bake their own bread, grow fruit and vegetables, and keep rabbits, a pig, chickens and bees. By this time Virginia had become an internationally acclaimed author, and alongside her writing she continued to work as a printer, binder and parcel dispatcher for Hogarth Press.

BEYOND THE WAVES

> *"Death is the enemy. Against you I will fling myself unvanquished and unyielding. O Death!"*
> **(the last line of Virginia Woolf's "The Waves" and her epitaph)**

In 1941, Virginia was once again suffering from severe depression and anorexia. The ever-present self-doubt in her abilities as a writer and the feeling of being inadequate as a wife were a constant source of torment.

But it was the loss of close family and friends and the destruction of their London homes that would eventually lead to her tragic demise.

At the end of March 1941, Virginia walked to the bank of the River Ouse, filled her pockets with stones and drowned herself. Her body was found three weeks later. After Virginia's death, Leonard continued his work for the Hogarth Press. Quentin Bell forged a career in education and worked as a crafter and potter. Angelica married Bunny Garnett, more than twenty years her senior and the former lover of her father Duncan Grant. Duncan continued his artistic career into old age.

Vanessa's pragmatic approach to life, that so often helped her to sail through adversity, made her continue to paint until her death in 1961.

Charleston, her evolving work of art for 45 years, has become her ultimate masterpiece.

Through obsession, sorrow, rivalry and love, the literary and artistic legacy of the two Stephen sisters has survived and remains strong to this day.

For further information about the Bloomsbury group and Charleston House visit **charleston.org.uk**

RATHER A TURN
FOR CORPSES

Georgia Corrick peers through
the spyglass at Detective
fiction of the 1930s

WORDS: **Georgia Corrick**
ADDITIONAL PHOTOS: **Freya Aspinall**

Picking up a newspaper in the nineteen-thirties, or listening to the wireless, could be perturbing. Unemployment was high, there were debates about malnutrition and slum clearances, worrying news from Germany and Ireland, hunger marches, fascist and anti-fascist meetings and demonstrations. On the other hand, people were working shorter hours for higher real wages, were beginning to have electrical appliances and even cars.

Detective fiction was becoming a national obsession. Four of my favourite writers began publishing detective series in the 1920s or 1930s: Dorothy Sayers, Patricia Wentworth, Ngaio Marsh and Michael Innes. They are part of the Golden Age of detective fiction.

I came across Michael Innes's books first, when I was about eleven. The language is heady for a child: formal and literary words like sequacious, nugatory, glyptic,

nescience, with abrupt changes to more direct language. There are digressions into art, architecture and sociology. The earlier books are often deliberately far-fetched, with exotic settings. In The Daffodil Affair (1942), one of Appleby's colleagues tells him:

> *"We're in a sort of hodge-podge of fantasy and harum-scarum that isn't a proper detective story at all. We might be by Michael Innes."*
> *"Innes? I've never heard of him." Appleby spoke with decided exasperation.*

In later books Appleby becomes more of an establishment figure as Sir John, Commissioner of Metropolitan Police. I spent much time as a child considering his career and trying to explain discrepancies in the timeline and events.

From Innes, I moved to Dorothy Sayers. Her detective, Lord Peter Wimsey, he of "I've got rather a turn for corpses", is more glamorous than Appleby: the wealthy son of a duke, moving between artistic and aristocratic worlds. Like Innes, Sayers often digresses to matters not directly related to the plot, such as the absorbing details of office life in Murder Must Advertise (1933).

The third detective series I loved as a child was Ngaio Marsh's Inspector Roderick Alleyn books. Marsh is a more sober writer than Innes or Sayers, but her ensemble casts of characters are great, particularly in the way she shows groups of people interacting – thrown together in theatrical settings, cults, art classes or house parties.

All three of these detectives are put on pedestals by their writers. Appleby specialises in making an entrance to grand country houses where things are in crisis. In Stop Press (1939) he arrives just as the lights have stopped working. drives his car on to the lawn to provide light, and replaces the fuse.

Lord Peter initially comes across as a bit of a fool, but quickly reveals that he is "a respectable scholar in five or six languages, a musician of some skill and more understanding, something of an expert in toxicology, a collector of rare editions", awarded a DSO during the War and a competent bell-ringer.

Roderick Alleyn is regarded with similar awe: characters "hero-worship" him, often after he has given them good advice. His police partner, Inspector Fox, flatters him:

"May I talk? And when I go wrong, Fox, you stop me."
"It's likely then,' said Fox dryly, 'to be a monologue ..."

I carried on reading, and re-reading, these books as an adult, and more recently found the Miss Silver series by Patricia Wentworth, also first published in the twenties and thirties. Miss (Maud) Silver is an ex-governess turned professional private detective. She's a compassionate woman to whom people are "glass-fronted". Wentworth is good on powerful and imperious women who dominate their families, like Agnes Fane in The Chinese Shawl (1943), and also on women who are trapped – by the expectations of their families, by sinister husbands or hypochondriacal parents.

Social class is an important issue for all these writers.

Lord Peter, although the most privileged of the detectives, has the most diverse range of acquaintances, even inviting a reformed burglar to his wedding. Marsh can be rather embarrassing to a modern reader about class. Witnesses are identified as "common" and people are constantly surprised and pleased to find "it is a help, Mr Alleyn being a gent" (Scales of Justice, 1958).

Despite the focus on poverty in the news in the 1930s, there is little recognition of poverty in these books. Of the four writers, Sayers is best at describing financial desperation. Police constable Joe Sellon keeps a wallet that he has found because "my wife was desperate bad after the baby – doctor said she ought to have special treatment – I hadn't saved nothing" (Busman's Honeymoon, 1937). And there is Captain Fentiman in The Unpleasantness at the Bellona Club (1928), who had a bad war and cannot find a job. The picture of his bitterness, misogyny and the difficulties in communication with his wife as a result of their poverty are well done.

Sayers, Wentworth and Marsh are good on details of everyday life of the time. Murders are often domestic, so in Death in Ecstasy (1936) the murderer makes sodium cyanide using a Fyrexo patent heat-proof crock and the poker. The maid spots that the poker has been filed down. Wentworth shows how disruptive murder can be to the routine of the house. In Latter End (1949) the cook thinks she is about to be arrested:

"if I'm took, you'll have to see to the lunch. There's the cold meat can go into a stew, and Polly can do the vegetables. That's a slow oven I've put the pudding in and you don't want to touch it."

The writers enjoy describing rooms – here is the parlour in Marsh's Plume of Feathers pub in Devon (Death at the Bar, 1940):

"Victoria's Jubilee and Edward the Seventh's wedding face each other across a small desert of linoleum and plush. Above the mantelpiece hangs a picture of two cylindrical and slug-like kittens. Upon the mantelpiece are three large shells. ... [And there is] a rag-rug."

Wentworth is excellent on village shops – I love this list of what the grocer sells: bacon, coffee, semolina, apples,

potatoes, root vegetables, twine, garden implements, shopping bags, boots, shoes and postcards (Miss Silver Comes to Stay, 1951).

Breakfast is a particular feature. Lord Peter has a string of excellent breakfasts, such as his servant dishing up kidneys and bacon, "glorious food, incomparable coffee [and] Oxford marmalade", compared to the meal his associate Detective Inspector Parker had been going to have, burnt porridge and cold tea served by his sneezing landlady (Clouds of Witness, 1926).

All four detectives have a strong ethical sense. Innes sees detection as part of a wider effort towards understanding, so Appleby says "Nothing really lasts, except the queer urge to make a little knowledge when one can" (Appleby Plays Chicken, 1956). Miss Silver says "There is no greater cause than justice, and in my humble

way I try to serve that cause" (The Key). Alleyn tells us;

"People interest me and homicide cases are so terrifically concerned with people" (Surfeit of Lampreys). He is sensitive, however, in Death in Ecstasy talking about how detection "makes monsters" of the police and "harpies" of the public, and just before the arrest in A Man Lay Dead (1934) saying that he finds it "almost intolerable". Lord Peter similarly finds arrests and punishment painful, but eventually accepts himself as a detective when Harriet tells him it's "your job, and it's worth doing" (Busman's Honeymoon).

My early reading of most of the novels I have talked about here has left me with a rag-bag of facts, memories and quotations, as well as multiple tatty copies of these

books in green Penguins or yellow Gollancz. I know
two methods of appearing to be a sheep when hunted
across a moor (The Secret Vanguard, 1940) and
that slates are categorised by size into large ladies,
countesses and duchesses (Innes, Hare Sitting Up,
1959). When playing bridge I remember Lord Peter's
advice that "There's many a man now walking the
streets of London … through not clearing trumps"
(Whose Body?, 1923). I know that when a document
is carelessly written it means that the author did
not care about the content (Have His Carcase, 1932)
and that the right way to correct small errors when
reviewing a book is in a private letter to the author
(Gaudy Night). My niece is Harriet partly after Harriet
Vane. Sayers wrote about "bringing all my actions and
opinions to the bar of [Lord Peter's] silent criticism"
(1937, quoted in Dorothy Sayers: Her Life and Soul,
Barbara Reynolds, 1998), and I find myself doing this
with all four detectives.

I have to acknowledge the problems with these
writers. They are all at times, racist, homophobic,
xenophobic, snobbish and misogynist, sometimes
startlingly so. Lucy Worsley writes that "One reason for
the great success of Golden Age detective fiction is that
it reflected the values of its readers right back at them –
and that image is not always an attractive one" (A Very
British Murder: The curious story of how crime was
turned into an art, 2013).

During the 1930s, the number of murders in
England and Wales averaged 318 a year – dwarfed by
the thefts of bicycles, just under 27 thousand a year.
Between them, Marsh, Innes, Sayers and Wentworth
certainly killed off more than a years' worth of victims.
It is reassuring to note that there is at least one bicycle
theft in the books (Five Red Herrings), even if this is an
under-representation of this epidemic. The argument
is that detective fiction, despite the horror of the deaths
and the disruption they cause, offered reassurance to a
society that had seen so much death in the First World
War and so much social change (case made for instance

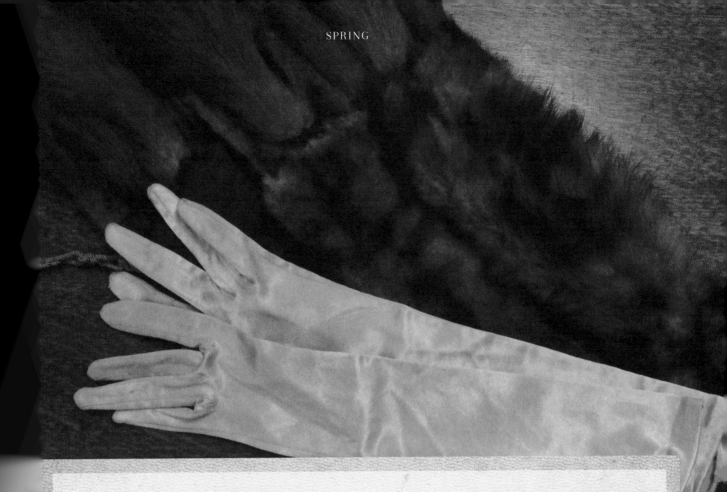

in Reflecting on Miss Marple, Marion Shaw and Sabine Vanacker, 1991). Margery Allingham, herself an excellent writer of detective fiction, similarly wrote that "the modern murder mystery [is] ... a sign of a popular instinct for order and form in a period of sudden and chaotic change". Miss Silver "diffuses an atmosphere of security which forbids" the recognition of crime ((The Gazebo, 1955) and Lord Peter "carried about with him that permanent atmosphere of security" (Busman's Honeymoon). There is an element of escapism too, of course. Sayers wrote that at a time of illness in her family, "The only person who remains cheerful and no nuisance to anybody is my Lord Peter" (quoted by Reynolds), and readers may have felt the same.

These four favourites of mine, and other Golden Age writers of detective fiction like Allingham, Josephine Tey, Agatha Christie, Edmund Crispin and Georgette Heyer, give us a window into 1930s Britain, and – if you read them at an impressionable age and as fortunate as I was – can change how we think of ourselves too.

WHERE TO START

Dorothy L Sayers: Clouds of Witness, 1926
Ngaio Marsh: Enter A Murderer, 1935
Michael Innes: Hamlet, Revenge! 1937
Patricia Wentworth: Lonesome Road, 1939

BLOGS FOR FURTHER READING

Classic Mysteries:
classicmysteries.net
Craig's Crime Watch:
kiwicrime.blogspot.co.uk
The Bodies from the Library:
thebodiesfromthelibrary.wordpress.com/ suggested-reading
The Passing Tramp:
thepassingtramp.blogspot.co.uk
The Wimsey Annotations:
planetpeschel.com/the-wimsey-annotations

Oh You Chicken!

Best Easter Wishes

WHILE~THE~CHICKENS~IN~THE~GARDEN,
KEEP~SCRATCHING~ALL~THE~TIME,
I~THOUGHT~YOU'D~LIKE~TO~HEAR~FROM~ME
SO~I'LL~SCRATCH~YOU~JUST~A~LINE.

A Happy Easter

EASTER HAPPINESS BE YOURS.

I bring you here an
EASTER nest
And wishes of the
very best.

103

BEAUTIFUL BOOKS

During the eighteenth century, ladies of high society kept handwritten notes on recipes and it became fashionable to exchange the most successful with friends and neighbours. This charming book is a compilation of fifty of the best recipes taken from the archives of the country houses of Britain and Ireland. Each recipe is shown in its original form accompanied by an up-to-date version created by professional chefs so that the recipes can be recreated today. In a world dominated by additives and synthetic foodstuffs, these traditional recipes contain only natural ingredients and show that simple ways are often the best when it comes to creating dishes that stand the test of time.

978-0-7509-6394-7   £15.00

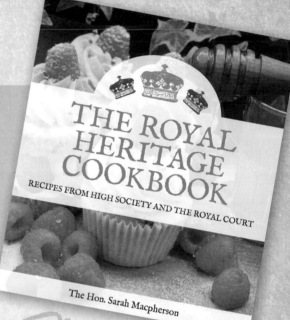

THE ROYAL HERITAGE COOKBOOK

RECIPES FROM HIGH SOCIETY AND THE ROYAL COURT

The Hon. Sarah Macpherson

THE RATION BOOK DIET

CAROL HARRIS, MIKE BROWN AND CJ JACKSON

Devised during the dark days of the Second World War, the wartime diet's low fat, high fibre and sensibly-sized portions meant that the British population enjoyed a level of health and fitness unsurpassed since 1945. Using the wartime diet as a model, *The Ration Book Diet* presents sixty recipes to enable you and your family to eat more healthily, together with interesting history of what it was like to live on rations.

978-0-7509-6822-5   £14.99

The Wartime Housewife will bring old fashioned values and skills to our very modern world! In this book, she shares recipes and tips on budgeting, repairing things, mending and scavenging; ideas for the school holidays, outings, gardening, DIY, sewing and craft; and anything else that might prove useful in your daily life. The Wartime Housewife knows only too well what it is like to manage on a tight budget and, by following her way, you too can learn to make the very best of what you have, as well as seeing the value in what is around you and making the most of it. Written with sharp wit and illustrated with vintage photographs, *Wartime Housewife* is the perfect guide to navigating gracefully the rigours of modern life.

978-0-7524-9109-7   £9.99

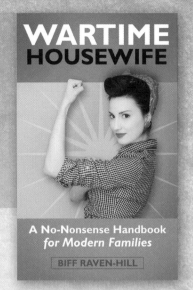

Drawing extensively on the little-known but important Suffragette Fellowship Collection of archive photographs, newspapers, personal correspondence, artefacts and memoirs, *Suffragettes in Pictures* presents a vivid picture of Suffragette life. With rare images of the Suffragette campaign leading to the outbreak of the First World War, the leading personalities in the Suffragette movement, such as Emmeline Pankhurst, Annie Kenney and Emily Wilding Davison, come to life.

978-0-7524-5796-3   £16.99

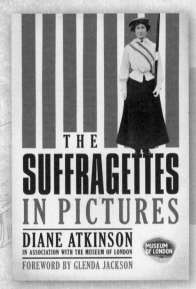

Pamela Jackson, née Mitford, is perhaps the least well known of the illustrious Mitford sisters, and yet her story is just as captivating, and more revealing. Despite shunning the bright city lights that her sisters so desperately craved, she was very much involved in the activities of her extraordinary family, picking up the many pieces when things went disastrously wrong – which they so often did. Joining her sisters on many adventures, including their meeting with Adolf Hitler in Nazi Germany, Pamela quietly observed the bizarre, funny and often tragic events that took place around her. Through her eyes, we are given a view of the Mitfords never seen before.

978-0-7509-6699-3   £9.99

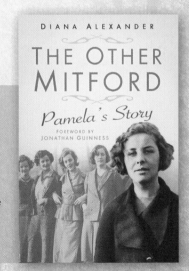

find these titles and browse for more ...

www.thehistorypress.co.uk

ACKNOWLEDGEMENTS

We have so many wonderful people to thank and without their co-operation and generous donations of their time and skills, this book would not have been possible.

Thank you to The National Trust for inviting us on a private behind the scenes viewing of the magnificent Red House. To Paul and Denny Welcomme for sharing their lovely home in Clevedon with us. To Kaffe Fassett for giving us your precious time for an interview,

and to the Quilters Guild for sharing their glorious collection with us. To the Charleston Trust for allowing us to use images of the beautiful Bloomsbury house in their care. To photographers Lyndsey James and Freya Aspinall for the use of your photographs.

A BIG thank you also goes to our families and friends who indulge us and understand us enough to know how important Pretty Nostalgic is to us.

CONTRIBUTORS

We would especially like to thank our Contributors:

SIBYLLE LAUBSCHER

Sibylle moved to the UK from Switzerland when she was 5. She studied Textile Design & Design Management and relocated to Vienna to work in investment banking, then a marketing director of a hosiery company. Returning to Switzerland in 2005, she is now an artist with a studio and shop, selling beautiful things. "Schöni Sache" "Schöni" – was the name of her grandfather's wheelwright business). She has a B&B, and in the garden live two chickens named Flame and Rapunzel by her children. *schoeni-sache.ch*

CORINNE YOUNG

Corinne is a Yorkshire-based textile artist specialising in embroidery. Her collections include floral artwork, garden themed interiors and large scale installations. She sees everything she makes as if it were a canvas to be embellished. Recycled materials and vintage ephemera feature strongly in her work. *corinneyoungtextiles.co.uk*

KATJA DELL

Part-time freelance illustrator and designer from Brighton. Her passion for Victoriana, fancy hats, burlesque theatre, ghost stories and decadent desserts is a constant source of inspiration for her work. When she is not creating quirky characters, she often scours flea markets and upcycles vintage furniture. *katjadell.com*

SEONA RILEY

Seona splits her time between rural Cheshire and the Lake District, where, if she's not concocting natural fragrance blends for her soaps and lotions, she's cycling rural country lanes, walking her dog Hector or crocheting colourful blankets. Her love of the Lakes is only topped by her love of rural New England, where she dreams of living in a log cabin in the woods someday. *villagealchemist.co.uk*

GABRIELA SZULMAN

Gabriela grew up in Buenos Aires, Argentina, but the neighbourhood of Camberwell in South London has been her home for many years now. She reassembles found images through collage and decoupage, and uses both these techniques to create pictures and upcycle anything from shoes to furniture. She finds inspiration in her grandmother's women's magazines, handwritten letters, Victoriana, technical manuals and illustrated dictionaries among other things. *gabrielaszulman.com*

SARAH MILLER WALTERS

Sarah is a writer with a passion for sewing – and she especially enjoys stitching items made from vintage maps. She finds the tiny pieces of poetry to be found in a Sylko cotton colour name very appealing and now runs a blog, which aims to record each one of them. Her favourite colour names are Gay Kingfisher and Buckingham Lilac. *sylkocolournamearchive. blogspot.co.uk*

GEORGIA CORRICK

Georgia researches and writes about domestic and women's history, Victorian and vintage children's books and vintage mysteries. She's writing her own 1930s mystery complete with fads of the time, gossip in the village post office and a poetry-quoting detective inspector. Her blog is at *booksandpictures. wordpress.com.*

NOSTALGIANEER PROFILE

Katja Dell

THE SWEET INDULGENCE OF THE TIME TRAVELLER

When I was 11 mum and I visited the Queen's Gallery at Buckingham Palace. I remember grinning broadly at the brightly-coloured paintings and feeling completely enveloped by the majestic gilded frames and the opulence of the place.

One of the walls displayed a collection of 17th Century miniatures by Samuel Cooper, and I fell head over heels in love with the portrait of the young Duke of Monmouth. Of the many historical crushes I experienced over the past decades (from Oscar Wilde to Prince Albert etc.), it was this one that made me want to hire a time machine.

Time travel is a soft and comforting blanket. And a journey back to lace, frills and petticoats is a sweet and harmless indulgence that transports me from a dull and sterile world to a time of beauty and chivalry.

In this modern desert of mindless consumerism, corporate culture and monochrome living, we are starting to develop a thirst for the values and traditions of times gone by.

The Pretty Nostalgic philosophy embodies these ideals perfectly and it has become an oasis for kindred spirits that are still able to appreciate the smell of a freshly published book or enjoy the visual feast of the Harrods Food Halls at Christmas, without resorting to their online catalogue.

MY CREATIVE JOURNEY SO FAR

I always enjoyed doodles, colours, patterns and textures. My initial love was photography, but I later re-trained in illustration and was awarded a Master of Arts in Sequential Design/Illustration from the University of Brighton in 2011, specialising in Picture Books for Children.

At present I am a part-time illustrator and I had the opportunity to exhibit at several local galleries, open houses and art shows. For the past few years I have been one of the resident artists at the Naughty Pirates Gallery on the Brighton seafront and was recently invited to join the Cobbled Lane Art collective in Barnham, West Sussex.

The ideas for my artwork come from my passion for burlesque theatre, period dramas, antiques, tattoo art, vampires, decadent puddings and anything remotely Victorian.

The dark humour of Tim Burton and the pop-surrealist universe of Mark Ryden have always provided an invaluable font of inspiration.

On cold winter evenings the marvellously crafted and chilling "Tales of Terror" by Chris Priestley never fail to boost my concentration during painting. My dream is to expand and print my collection of images on toys, stationary and kitchenware, publish a picture book or write a historical biography.

Most of my weekends are spent sipping tea with a Baron, scouring vintage markets and up-cycling second-hand furniture. Over the years I have accumulated an insane amount of books and knick-knackery and my interest will always be aroused by quirky objects that possess warmth and personality and a Pretty Nostalgic feel.

ISSUE TWO Meet the couple decorating their home with found furniture; collect vintage picnic sets; meet Wayne Hemingway and a kitsch ice cream maker; learn how to paint shabby chic furniture; decorate your home with natural history trinkets and try out victory rolls.

ISSUE THREE Celebrate British wool makers; make hedgerow cocktails; go on two-wheeled adventures and collect antique sewing machines; share Alys Fowler's love for jams and chutneys, rediscover the lost joys of tree climbing and create a community garden.

ISSUE FOUR Buy British made party frocks and suits, choose locally-made stocking fillers, make a winter wreath from hedgerow finds, collect vintage baubles, celebrate life's simple pleasures, mull wine and fill your pockets with shells.

ISSUE FIVE Peek inside a houseboat; collect vintage cameras; challenge your expectations at the all new Women's Institute; learn how to make paper and dig for victory like a homefront gardener; enter the miniature world of doll's houses and indulge in a love of typography.

ISSUE SEVEN Sell art from your front room; create a memory capsule; discover ancient wedding traditions and grow miniature salads; marvel at a menagerie of creatures, and collect ephemera; meet Jules Hudson, try Lindy Hop and discover underground supper clubs.

ISSUE EIGHT Learn the history of vintage swimwear; make a banquet of edible flowers; collect postcards; celebrate British piers; enter our storytelling competition; enjoy barefoot walking; indulge in natural spa remedies and renovate your dream vintage caravan.

ISSUE NINE Discover the thrills of wild straw-pressed cider; reap the medicinal benefits of elderberries; cosy up with a jam jar craft project; read George Clarke's tips on creating a garden bolt hole; peek into the life of a 1950s Woman's Journal fashion editor and learn how to keep bees.

ISSUE TEN Plan a Dickensian feast; explore the Cotswold sanctuary of one of Britain's most prolific collectors; treat yourself to some seriously saucy British-made lingerie; slip into the bawdy world of Music Hall and delight in a love of bold, bright kitchenalia.

ISSUE ELEVEN Naturally clean your home; see a gardening revolution; build your own house; learn the history of wartime rationing; discover the fate of the great auk and the secrets of vintage makeup; visit secret gardens; explore British shoemakers and signwriters; discover potting.

ISSUE TWELVE Bursting with the joys of spring, discover: traditional house cleaning methods; up-cycling old board games; men who collect tanks; homeopathic remedies; how to find fairy folk; vintage dress patterns; make raw chocolate and cook with eggs.

ISSUE THIRTEEN Visit a ceramic gallery; scour the shoreline; remember forgotten brands; collect vinyl; forage for food; read out loud; keep young and beautiful using natural ingredients; visit North Norfolk; peek inside a showman's caravan; learn the history of homemade ice cream and discover how to mince.

COMPENDIUM ONE: Memories of childhood toys; a history of Jigsaws; collecting vintage buttons, and treasuring Teddy Bears. Home-made hair care; a guide to using vintage sewing machines; Bristol Wood Recycling Project. Classic British Movies, Alice in Wonderland and discovering Brighton.

HOME

This book will inspire you to look at the way you view your home and how you live in it. To furnish your home with things you love and things that will last. It won't cost the earth or put you in debt, but it will be a happy home.

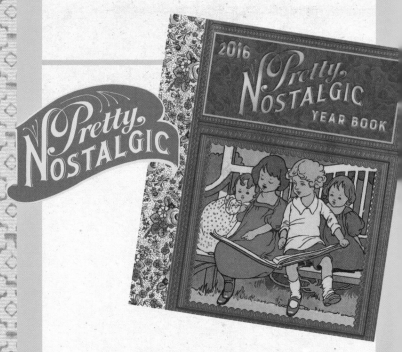

YEAR BOOK 2016

This is a traditional style annual for grownups that appreciate traditional things. It contains vintage living hints and tips all year around including lots of recipes, crafts and upcycling ideas. Every page is beautifully designed and illustrated and joyful look at as well as to read.

THE PRETTY NOSTALGIC COMPENDIUM - SPRING 2016

A Pretty Nostalgic® Publication
11 Acland Road, Bridgend,
Mid Glamorgan, CF31 1TF
Text copyright © Nicole Burnett 2016

*Nicole Burnett has asserted her right to be identified as
the author of this work in accordance with the copyright,
designs and patents Act, 1988.*

*A Catalogue record of this book is available from the
British Library and the National Library of Wales.*

ISBN 978-0-7509-6775-4

Concept, text, editorial and image sourcing
Nicole Burnett
Styling
Nicole Burnett and Rae Edwards
Design, photography and illustration
Rae Edwards
Publisher
Sophie Bradshaw, The History Press
Published by The History Press
The Mill, Brimscombe Port
Stroud, Gloucestershire GL5 2QG
thehistorypress.co.uk

Content © Pretty Nostalgic Ltd 2016

Printed in Great Britain